W9-BTK-606

No Ticket? No Problem!

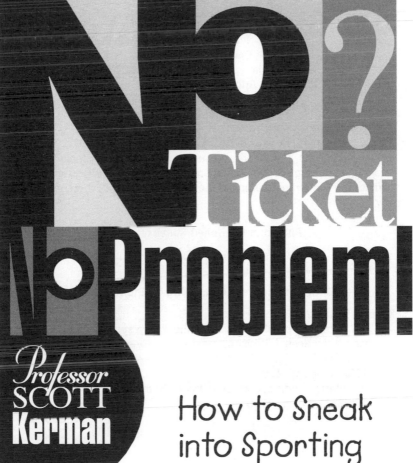

No Ticket Problem!

Professor SCOTT Kerman

How to Sneak into Sporting Events and Concerts

THE SUMMIT PUBLISHING GROUP • ARLINGTON, TEXAS

THE SUMMIT PUBLISHING GROUP
One Arlington Centre
1112 East Copeland Road, Fifth Floor
Arlington, Texas 76011

Copyright © 1996 by Scott Kerman

All rights reserved. No part of this book may be reproduced or transmitted in any form or by any means, electronic or mechanical, including photocopying, recording, or by any information storage and retrieval system, without the written permission of the publisher, except where permitted by law.

Printed in the United States of America.

00 99 98 97 96   040   5 4 3 2 1

Library of Congress Cataloging-in-Publication Data

Kerman, Scott J., 1966–
    No ticket? No problem! : how to sneak into sporting events and concerts / by Scott J. Kerman.
        p. cm.
    ISBN 1-56530-226-5
    1. Entertainment events—Admission—Humor.   I. Title.
    PN6231.E64K47 1996
    818'.5407—dc20   96-35680
                                                                                            CIP

Cover and book design by David Sims

*This book is dedicated to
the greatest parents in the universe,
Norman and Shirley Kerman.
Thank you for everything. All my love.*

*I dedicate it also to Leslie, a true angel;
Bryan, the best older brother a guy could ask for;
and Tracy, Jeff, Rob, and Robbie, Jr.,
for their constant support.*

*Special thanks to
Keith and Candy for their time, advice, and editing.
Thanks also to my best friend, Robert Lubeck.*

*With love to my partner in crime,
Adrienne Arrage.*

*This book is in remembrance of my grandmothers,
Rose G. Bagdoian and Bessie Kerman.
You are always in my thoughts.*

Contents

Lecture 9

Lecture 10

Lecture 11

Lecture 12

Lecture 13

Final Exam:

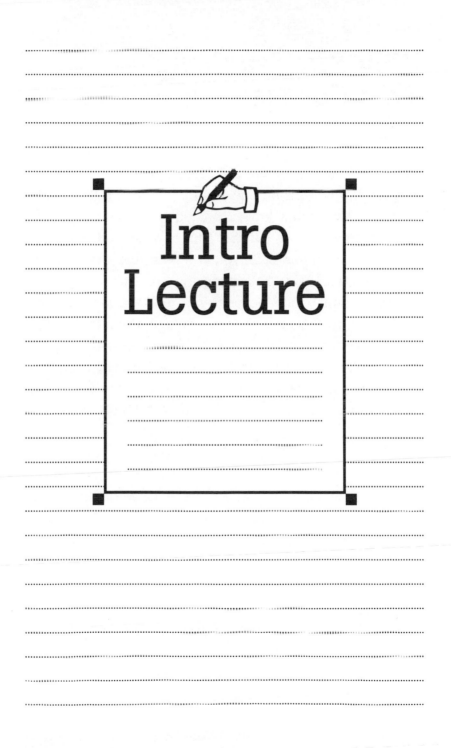

Intro Lecture

Why I'm Teaching This Course

Professor Scott J. Kerman, B.S.: Hello! Welcome to my class, "Introductory Lessons on Sneaking into Sporting Events and Concerts." My name is Professor Scott Kerman, and I will be your teacher. Now, settle down. This is a required course.

By the end of this class, you will be able to attend sporting events and concerts without the hassles of long ticket lines, busy signals, outrageous prices, or sacrificing your firstborn. You will attend lots of entertainment events and always get your money's worth.

I expect everyone in this class to read carefully or wait for the video, laugh loudly, and cheat on the tests. Now, slouch back in your seats and try to retain something other than water.

I'm Just a Gigolo!

■ I am teaching this class as a representative of the average person, whose love and need for entertaining sporting events and concerts are extreme, but whose wealth and power are limited.

Ticket prices these days are out of control. At fifty dollars to see a football game or three hundred dollars to see a top concert, attending a sporting event or concert is becoming a once-in-a-lifetime event.

Is it any wonder that old-time rock-and-roll bands are getting back together? At sixty bucks a head, band members can afford to get along.

In twenty years, they'll have to wheel out Mick Jagger for the Stones summer tour. Instead of singing "I can't get no satisfaction," Mick will be singing, "I can't get my food down."

Of course, the professional athletes are constantly going on strike. How, after all, are the players expected to raise a family of four on $2 million a year for working six months a year?

It's Good to Be a Wiener!

■ In teaching this class, let me emphasize that no harm is being done to the owners of the teams or stadiums. I know you have sleepless nights worrying about those billionaires.

First of all, owners make most of their profits in concessions sales. All of you who work long and hard sneaking in will certainly be hungry and thirsty. Happily, you'll buy overpriced food, drinks, and souvenirs.

Class, an economics lesson . . . No, please don't leave. You won't be asked to add anything.

Do you know the profit margin on a four-dollar hot dog? I'm guessing $3.95, and that includes unlimited relish. And how much exactly is the one piece of notebook paper it takes to make the seven-dollar painter's cap?

Hearts be warmed, class, the owners' profit margins will not be hurt. Actually, the owners will be helped.

The seats you'll sit in, class, will be empty. This is a great service to the owners. Empty seats degrade the importance of the event. Thanks to you, when the camera pans the crowd the announcer will remark, "There isn't an empty seat in the house."

Your Mom Wears Army Boots!

■ In fact, during the annual broadcast of the Academy Awards, people are hired to sit in the seats of presenters and award winners, so the television audience never sees an empty seat. What type of qualifications do you need for this job? Do you just have to have a better attitude than your average mannequin?

At many events, spectators are disguised as plastic chairs. You will be asked to occupy those embarrassing gaps.

We will also raise the noise levels. Our loud and constant commentary regarding visiting players' mothers and their dietary habits will provide a helpful distraction for the home team.

During concerts, you will cough your lungs out expressing love for the music. This will, if it is at all humanly possible, inflate the egos of the musicians, and the music videos will look awesome.

If you think about it, and I understand thinking is painful, the sports owners and concert promoters should be grateful I am teaching this class.

Anybody Have a Telestrator?

■ In this class, I will analyze all aspects of sporting events and concerts. We will look at the different groups of people that you'll meet at events and figure out whom to seek out and whom to avoid. I will explain my proven strategies for getting into events, tell you what not to try, and even show you how to get the best seats.

I'll also share my personal stories and the stories of some talented people versed in the art of sneakery. Now, take out your notebooks—doodle if you must. It's time to get a real education.

Lecture

1

The Event

Student: How do we sneak in, Professor?

Professor: Good question, you little brownnose. We will cover that later. Our first challenge, however, is to get to the event. Although this seems easy, it isn't.

Public transportation could be an answer. Unfortunately, most new stadiums and arenas are built in deserted suburbs where the only form of public transportation is to be carted away by the police.

Hitchhiking is another option. Are any of you taking sociology class? Who's scarier—the hitchhikers or the people who pick them up? In fact, 90 percent of all hitchhikers have a criminal record and the other 10 percent haven't been caught yet.

The most popular option, of course, is to drive. If you don't own an automobile, borrow one. I don't endorse stealing a car. However, if you possess this uncanny ability, I suggest returning the car to its proper owner immediately after the event... well, maybe just one postgame party. Remember, though, refill the gas tank and remove the empties. It's the little things that count.

Free Parking Is an Inalienable Right!

■ Parking prices at the event range from five dollars to twenty dollars. At Fenway Park in Boston, it costs twenty bucks to park. If the car isn't worth that much, you might persuade the attendant to take ownership.

At big city stadiums, I recommend a couple of ways to avoid paying parking.

The first strategy is to park on the street. In the city, there should be residential or metered parking.

With residential parking, you need a residential parking sticker on your car to park over a certain time limit. Write a note and leave it on the windshield explaining how you moved into the area yesterday and will be getting a parking permit tomorrow. This works like a charm.

As for parking meters, my suggestion is to write "out of order" on the meter and go your merry way. Use a black magic marker—it looks official—and write "Badge No. 872." All inspectors have numbers instead of names; how personal! This will confuse the ticket writers enough to move on to their next victim.

Free parking is provided to media personnel. We will teach you later how to sneak into the event as a press person, but regarding parking, just drive up to the gate and tell them you're with the media. You'll be directed to the choice parking lot.

If you have friends who work at a funeral home (not your typical party animals), drive up to the event in a hearse. Speak in a low tone, dress like Uncle Fester of the Addams Family, and drench yourself in ammonia. Explain to the parking attendant that you're there to pick up the body. If he asks what body, tell him the one they just found in the stadium. You'll get right through, and the attendant will be the jerk

who started the bogus rumor about a dead guy at the event.
Student: Great, Professor. Now that we're at the event, isn't it time to teach us how to sneak in?
Professor: Remember, class, participation can hurt your grade, too.

Four Score and Seven Events Ago!

■ Everybody likes to beat the system. Millions of people cheat on their taxes and have little or no remorse—Pete Rose is not so much remorseful as pissed off. And all of us have jaywalked a time or two. Does this make us bad people?... No.
Student: Then, Professor, what are the reasons law-abiding citizens break the rules?
Professor: Finally, a student with a good question. You're dismissed.

The first and most alluring reason, class, is money. As my father says, "The issue is not the money; the truly important issue is the Money!"

In these tough economic times, people barely scrape out a living. You can't spend what you don't have unless, of course, you have a credit card. But the public's need to be entertained is greater than ever. Cable television is now more important than owning a bed in many homes, and video stores are on every block.

Watching a sporting event or concert live and in person, however, remains a thrill everyone should have the opportunity to enjoy.
Student: Does this mean that due to lack of funds, one's morals and values are compromised?

Professor: The answer, class, is a most definite yes! If we were all rich and powerful, we would be sipping umbrella drinks at the beach and hanging out in luxury box seats with the beautiful people.

In reality, we consider a seat luxurious if the person behind us spills only one beer during the event, and no ten-year-old is kicking us in the back.

Buy Me a Drink and I'm Yours for the Evening!

■ Rich and powerful people can afford to have morals... or the alternative, a good attorney. The rest of us replace morals with standards.

How do I best describe standards? I always say I never go out with a girl who doesn't meet my standards. Until I meet a girl, then I just lower them.

Listen to this from Andy Staursk, a U.S. Steel publicist... Class, I am now quoting someone. Hint: This is usually on the test. "On Monday morning, you can find a president of a Fortune 500 company, a salesman, and a maintenance man in front of the U.S. Steel building talking football, and from the way they talk there would be no way in the world to distinguish their stations in life."

What does this quote mean, class? Yes, you, with the pencil in your belly button.

Student: Uhh, that no matter what your standing in life is, one can have equal knowledge of sports?

Professor: Correct. However, the Fortune 500 guy has a bigger television set and a better food spread. So, don't hesitate to agree with his opinion, especially if he's inviting you over to watch the game.

We Got to the Event in One Piece; Now What?

■ Okay, we have now arrived at our destination. The event! Sporting events and concerts are held in two places. Class, the answer is stadiums and arenas.

Stadiums are large, mostly open facilities with lots of outlets for sneaking in. Arenas accommodate indoor sports and most concerts and are smaller than stadiums. We will have an equal chance to sneak into stadiums and arenas. But, because stadiums are bigger, there are more gates to execute our plans.

Are You a Member of a Food Group?

■ Outside the event you will see three groups of people. The first group has tickets to the event. These people possess permanent, shit-ass grins on their faces... What? Hey, this is college. Professors are allowed to curse once in a while! These people are organized, pay their taxes, have dates, a clean home, and a bright future. You'll find they answer to names like Biff, Travis, Courtney, or Snookums.

We despise this group. We must ignore them, because we cannot relate to them. This is what Reggie Jackson says about the nonbaseball fans who always get tickets for a World Series: "Did you ever see true baseball fans showing up for a game in three-piece suits, evening gowns, and furs? The real fan is the one without a shirt who shouts obscenities at the players, especially when they make an error or do not sign autographs."

Good old Mr. October. Now that he's in the Baseball Hall of Fame, he's worthy of legendary status and a question on the final exam. Hint.

The second group consists of the people looking for tickets.

Student: Yo, Prof! That's us guys, right?

Professor: No, Rocky junior. We are different, because we are educated. This second group is separated into two categories.

The first are people with lots of money to spend who are willing to pay anything to see the event. They're commonly known as suckers. They deal exclusively with scalpers, whom I will discuss in a moment.

The rest are people who have little or no money and are looking for divine intervention to get a ticket. You can relate to this group. These people are fans.

Partridge Family Clubs Brady Bunch to Death!

■ Which is defined as what, class? Okay. Jan, of *Brady Bunch* fame.

Student: A fan is a person who uses a device to produce a current of air.

Professor: Who let her in? Jan, honey, why don't you go outside and see if you can find where your career went.

A fan is an enthusiastic supporter or spectator of a sport or of some form of the arts. It is short for fanatical, which means potential wacko.

These people get a thrill just being outside the event. They are also the only people who buy cotton candy and 7-Eleven pizza.

I remember talking with a woman at a Rod Stewart concert who was psyched to be in the same area code as Rod. After a few minutes listening to this groupie, it became clear she was the only one located in her area code.

I'm a Recovering Groupie!

■ There are two types of groupies. Music groupies are mostly women who, in exchange for partying and hanging out with the band, will provide sexual favors upon request to band members.

Groupies wear lots of leather and ten-inch-heel shoes and give prostitutes a bad name. The dream of all men is to have these groupies slinking around their back doors one day.

During concerts, you may notice security guards handing young pretty women backstage passes to recruit a new bevy of groupies. Clearly, the National Organization for Women hasn't passed out literature at concert halls as of yet.

What good is it to be a rock star without groupies? After hearing fifty thousand women screaming your name during a concert, do you really want to hang out later with your mom while she tells you to get a haircut?

Will Kill for Autographs!

■ Sports groupies consist of forty-five-year-old guys who carry autograph books around, still use pencils, and write down stuff on hamburger wrappers. They have bumper stickers on suitcases, wear shorts in the winter, have big asses, and stink.

They bore you with endless stories of jobs lost and women never found. It's depressing to watch because, with the wrong prescribed medicine or bad diet, we can easily become one of them.

They hang around the stadiums for hours before and after the game trying to catch a glimpse of a player. When the team's on the road, these people fill their time in the studio audiences for talk shows like *Ricki Lake*.

Dealing with this dysfunctional group is the only time I feel sorry for overpaid athletes. The idea of a crazy man at my place of work every day, screaming to me how much he loves me and how good I look in my uniform, is downright frightening.

Why Scalpers Suck!

■ The people—and I use this word loosely—you will have the most unsolicited contact with are scalpers. Scalpers play a role in the lack of availability of tickets for an event. Class, I must address the subject of scalpers at length.

Scalpers are local hoods who gobble up thousands of tickets to events and sell them outside at exorbitant prices.

As you might have noticed, the same faces are present outside every event, hoping to sell tickets. When a ticket goes on sale for big events, most of the people in line are scalpers. There are, as you know, some diehards who will do anything to get a ticket. But, in large part, these are professional scalpers scooping up as many tickets as possible.

This group of rejects—the bottom of the organized crime food chain—sells tickets for as much as fifty times the original prices.

I remember the 1993 Super Bowl in Pasadena, which pitted Dallas against Buffalo. A Dallas fan, distinguished by his ten-gallon hat, use of "y'all" as an adjective, and his beautiful "secretary" (right!) at his side, paid a scalper five thousand dollars for two tickets worth a total of three hundred bucks. I imagine that the secretary had worked really hard that week, and her appreciative boss was rewarding her.

Scalpers are not to be confused with private ticket agencies. These are legal scalpers who avoid arrest by use of the creative words *service charge*.

Ticket agents are scalpers with an address. Organizations such as Ticketmaster, the largest ticketing agency, practically have a monopoly on rock-concert ticket sales.

Fans buying tickets through these agencies pay on average five to eight dollars per ticket in service charges. A lot of stadiums have exclusive contracts with these price gougers. If you want to buy a ticket, you're forced to pay their prices.

Eddie Vedder is the Antichrist!

■ The rock band Pearl Jam testified in Washington D.C. at a House Government Operations Subcommittee investigation into the high service charges of ticket agencies. People were most impressed that the members of the group combed their hair.

Scalpers are very crafty con artists who give the consumer the impression that every event is all sold out. However, if the

Atlanta Falcons are playing the Tampa Bay Buccaneers, it is a safe bet that good seats are available.

There are many negative points to buying tickets from scalpers.

First, it allows the lazy bums to stay on the street—when not inside shoplifting—and to spend your hard-earned money on illegal substances.

Second, it gives them gas money to drive to the welfare office. For a number of people, welfare is a nice "second" income.

In addition, there is a distinct possibility that you are dealing with a person who is far from honest. Criminals tend to be this way. You may lose more than cash—like your watch or scalp.

Scalpers will also con you into believing that their seats are close to the stage or in the middle of the field. In reality, the seats are usually a huge disappointment.

If you're in New York and the seats are in Maine, they are in a bad section. You will likely be behind a pole or overhang or in the nosebleed seats. There's a greater chance you'll see mountain goats or share peanuts with people in airplanes than see the participants in the event.

Rip-Off Artists!

■ Class, I have a story to tell. No, Bubba. You cannot sit on my lap.

While attending an Aerosmith concert, I met a couple who had purchased tickets from a scalper for $175 each. When they went to the entrance gate, the ticket taker informed them that the tickets were counterfeit. The scalper had suckered a number of unsuspecting people with this counterfeit ticket scam.

This is a very common story at events, which teaches a valuable lesson. If you're going to use bogus tickets, make them yourself instead of paying hundreds of dollars for them.

Another bad ticket story occurred when I was in San Francisco for an N.F.C. Championship game. Two San Francisco 49ers fans bought tickets from a scalper. Ten minutes later, having studied the tickets closely, the fans realized they were last year's play-off tickets.

The only way in for those guys was to land in the Twilight Zone and go back to last year's game. I think I saw them calling Rod Serling for advice.

You'll Never Take Me Alive!

■ There's one last problem with scalpers. The person you believe is a scalper could be an undercover cop. Scalping is illegal in most states, and trying to buy a scalped seat can get you in trouble.

Actually, getting arrested for being a john in the prostitution of tickets is rare. The police are hoping to arrest the scalpers and confiscate the tickets. Unfortunately, scalpers never do any real jail time.

What a shame! They're given a small fine and a slap on the wrist. As for the tickets? Well, let's just say the families and friends of law enforcement are some of pro sports' best fans.

At this time, class, we'll have a snack break. Before you go, let me remind you of my fetish for cupcakes, which is the energy source I prefer when grading final exams... Why, thank you, Larry.

Student: My name is Harry.

Professor: Whatever. I'm just impressed with your initiative, quick decision-making ability, and kiss-up skills. You're definitely an A student, Barry.

A Blimp Shot Would Be Helpful.

■ Back to our lesson. We have become familiar with the different groups of people at the event. Our next goal is to understand the surroundings.

We must take on the role of Green Berets (how scary can guys wearing green visorless caps really be?) and go on a reconnaissance mission of the stadium or arena.

To fulfill our mission, we must arrive at the event as early as possible. If this means leaving work early and risking future employment, so be it. "Seize the day!" That's "carpe diem" for the foreign-speaking audience.

Arriving at an event early expands your options for sneaking in. Walk around the stadium and familiarize yourself with the locations of the entrances and other potential places to sneak in. We will cover all of them in this class.

Student: Does this mean you're finally going to teach us how to sneak in?

Professor: Very soon, but preparation is a large part of success. Class, what makes a doctor successful? The answer is patience and more patience. No pun intended.

Students: Boo! Boo!

Professor: The natives are getting restless. Nevertheless, we must now focus on a very important element of sneaking in—attitude.

Having an Attitude Is Good!

■ Webster's Dictionary has two good definitions of attitude: "1. A position of the body or manner of carrying oneself, indicative of a mood or condition. 2. A state of mind or feeling with regard to some matter: disposition."

Student: Hey, Professor. What makes this guy Webster the authority on the English language?

Professor: I don't know. I guess he has a good publisher. Class, did you know the Webster dictionary was originally released as a satire but, due to limited sales, was re-released as a reference guide?

Student: Then what about the words he didn't know the meanings for?

Professor: Some guy named Thesaurus helped him out.

Back to attitude. When sneaking into events, you must exude confidence and give the impression that you belong. When dealing with stadium personnel, never entertain any suggestion that your story is questionable. Always express shock if there is resistance.

Remember, you belong in the stadium, and security personnel are a small nuisance that people who belong in the stadium for free must face. If you can keep this mind-set, you will be highly effective.

I Need Makeup!

■ You'll need good acting skills to convince people you're something you're not. I practice with this one—"Ma, I'm not a bum, I'm just finding myself."

If you can convince yourself you are that particular character, you can convince others. "Oh, honey, let the bum find himself." Thanks, Mom. So, no matter what strategy you are pursuing, have a positive attitude.

Class, I think you've been briefed enough about our covert operation. I will now reveal to you the paths of entry and strategies for infiltrating stadiums and events. We have arrived at the Main Event. So LET'S GET READY TO RUMBLE!!

Student A: What'd he say? What'd he say?

Student B: Who knows? Just cheer. He may be dangerous!

Class: Hooray!

The Top 11
Easiest Stadiums to Sneak Into

··

And the losers are:

11. **Baltimore's Camden Yards**—"Mr. Gehrig, here to see Mr. Ripken."

10. **Dallas Cowboys Stadium**—Security guards' IQs are lower than Forrest Gump's.

9. **The Seattle Kingdome**—Once you're in, you realize you're at a nuclear waste site.

8. **Philadelphia's Veterans Stadium**—Easy to sneak in; tough to find a seat that doesn't bite.

7. **Chicago's United Center**—Yes, it's true, I'm Michael Jordan's love child.

6. **Los Angeles Dodgers Stadium**—Sneak in late, sneak out early.

5. **New Jersey Meadowlands**—Hoffa snuck in and never left.

4. **Boston's Fenway Park**—Punishment for free entry is lifelong curse of being a Red Sox fan.

3. **Miami's Joe Robbie Stadium**—Just don't ever let them see you sweat.

2. **The Anaheim Pond**—"I'm Mr. Mickey Mouse. Where do I go?"

1. **U.S. Air Arena**—Gives new meaning to "open to the public."

Lecture

2

Methods of Entry: The Service Gate

I am now going to discuss the specific entrances into a stadium. By understanding the gates and the people who use them, you can impersonate these people and join the festivities.

I Need to Be Serviced!

■ The first path of entry is the *service gate*. The service gate is the entrance used by stadium personnel.

Personnel such as the ushers (or seating engineers as they are often called), ticket takers, security guards, concessionaires, maintenance people, and event personnel gain access through these gates.

Depending on the stadium security policy, these employees may possess employee identification. Not all stadiums require this, however, which is a great help to the potential infiltrator.

Ushers and concessionaire employees enter the stadium from two and a half to three hours before the scheduled event's starting time.

Most stadiums make the employees gather outside the gate and enter all at once. This is similar to a buffalo stampede. In fact, after they enter, someone has to spread sawdust in the spots they gathered. A gate monitor will glance quickly at the identifications and they're in the door.

Here, students, is your first opportunity to sneak into the event. I want you to join this elite group of food and seating soldiers.

Remember, in the course of any covert operation, we must be kind to people who have top-secret information. Of course, never get too close to these people, or you could possibly compromise the whole operation and the national defense of this great country.

Get Your Red Hots Here!

■ Strike up a conversation with a concessionaire. They tend to be younger and more willing to give out information. Ushers tend to be old, bitter, and sick of pointing. Ushers will play a role in our operation, however, so while hanging out with the concessionaires, write down a couple of the ushers' names and say "Hello."

Have the vendor, alias "concessionaire," show you his employee identification card. Most of the stadium identifications are bad-picture IDs similar to a college ID or driver's license.

Class, let me see some of your driver's licenses. My theory is correct. No one in the country has ever taken a good driver's license picture. Even the few of you who are attractive look like police sketches.

If the employee ID is similar to any of your IDs—college, work, even baby pictures—then our first attempt will be to enter with the vendors, while quickly showing the ID.

When you get to the monitor, have the ID in your wallet and, matter-of-factly, show as little of the ID as possible.

Make sure to distract the monitor's attention. Usually, these people have the concentration levels of lobsters. A simple "How you doing?" should break his train of thought and you'll breeze right through.

Wanted Dead or Alive!

■ Class, let me tell you of my greatest accomplishment concerning concessions: the 1996 Super Bowl held at Sun Devil Stadium in Phoenix, Arizona, between the Dallas Cowboys and the Pittsburgh Steelers.

The Friday before the game, the story of my great talent was chronicled in our nation's newspaper, the *USA Today* sports page—the newspaper with few words and great pictures.

The article had a picture of me and some tips from my class. Also a quote from NFL security honcho Jim Steeg saying, "Mr. Kerman will have his work cut out for him; it's a challenge. There's tons of security and tons of checks, constant checks."

From these comments, you understand two things: Security would be looking for me and Mr. Steeg likes the word *ton.*

Mr. Bluffman to the Rescue!

■ The article referred to me as Mr. Bluffman—in the same vein as Superman, Batman, and Underdog. Mr. Bluffman, able to leap over tall ticket booths in a single bound, more powerful than a speeding security guard. Look up in the sky—it's a media person, it's a peanut vendor, no, it's Bluffman!!

On game day, I put my game face on. I had found out on Saturday night that the *USA Today* article was being posted to every security wall so that all security personnel would be on the lookout for me. I was even mentioned in the briefing of employees on the day of the game!

With all the exposure, I knew I had to wear a disguise. As I told you, class, I'm Armenian, and if I don't shave for an hour I have a beard. So I didn't shave for four days. By Sunday, I looked hairier than Chewbacca.

I went to the stadium eight hours early to scope out the place. I walked around the stadium a number of times to see what would be the easiest chance of intervention. I noticed a shuttle bus dropping off concessionaires at the stadium for work. The lightbulb in my head shined bright.

After the bus emptied, I asked the driver if I could get a ride to wherever she picked up these people. She agreed and drove me twenty-five minutes outside the stadium to a parking lot in the desert.

A sign-up tent was set up, and unless you had a job that day you would never have known this was out here. I walked around the parking lot looking for my window of opportunity. Suddenly, I heard a woman screaming, "I need hot dog vendors! I need hot dog vendors!"

This Class Saves Lives!

■ I went over to the woman in distress and introduced myself as Mr. Oscar Mayer. She laughed and asked if I had ever served hot dogs before—as if this is a special skill or something! I told her I went to Hot Dog University for a year and then transferred to Chocolate Eclair University.

She asked if I had filled out an application. I said they lost it and she remarked that I wasn't the first. The hot dog vendor bus was filling up, so she quickly handed me a visor, polyester shirt, and a pass to full access to the stadium. It worked!! I jumped on the bus and went into the stadium.

As I entered the stadium, I saw a scalper get six thousand dollars for two tickets. I was in the Super Bowl for free and had been given vouchers for free pretzels and soda. I went looking for a phone booth to call the *USA Today* reporter to follow up for the Monday edition.

The phone booth I used was next to police services! As I was calling, I looked through the window and I could see the *USA Today* article on me posted on the wall. I was a marked man!! I made the call and scooted out of sight.

Oh, about the game; the rinky-dink Sun Devil Stadium only has benches, so I sat at the fifty-yard line squeezing between the numbers eighteen and nineteen. The people were nice enough to let me sit there because I was the guy who could get free hot dogs the whole game.

It was a great day and a complete success. *USA Today* had a big story in the next day's paper. The headline read "Pro Gate Crasher Adds to his Super Reputation." Class, if this doesn't get the chicks, I don't know what will.

What is Relish?

■ Some stadium identification cards have no pictures. If this is the case, a Triple A or any laminated card can be used. I wonder if getting laminated can be performed on an outpatient basis?

A borrowed ID is the easiest way in. If you have befriended someone who can be trusted and who has worked at the stadium for more than two days, find out if he knows the person at the gate. If he does, ask to borrow his ID (since he won't need it anyway). If you're not using a legitimate ID and there is any kind of problem at the gate (e.g., the monitor notices that you are allowed to check out Hemingway but not the event with that particular card), calmly explain that you must have left your ID at home and that you sell soft drinks. This is plenty of information, and you will be let in.

Remember, the turnover rate for these positions is pretty high. The stadium officials are never too familiar with the vendors. There aren't too many gold watches given out in the concessions business. If you've worked a week, you're considered a veteran and eligible for a Casio.

Having a job as a vendor is like being a farmhand on the old western television shows. Remember, the farmhands would work one week at *Bonanza* and then have to go the next week to the *Big Valley*. It's the same principle in this work world. I miss the old westerns; can you imagine John Wayne using a handheld rocket launcher to shoot Indians?

Try to have the person you befriended go before you in line, and maintain a lively conversation when you're near the checkpoint. If there is lots of laughter, this will entertain the monitor enough to forget his limited responsibilities.

If there is any problem, your new friend can vouch for you. As my grandma says, you'll be "In like Flynn."

My Shirt is the Color of a Carnival Tent!

■ The vendors have uniforms. They're either kept at the stadium or in people's gym bags until they get into the event. Due to their attractive colors—colors usually reserved for dishcloths and golf pants—no one who wants to have a date will wear these 100 percent polyester uniforms out in public.

The vendors have hats, which some wear when entering the stadium. The people wearing these unattractive hats are generally having a very bad hair day or have no hair.

If the person you have befriended does not appear to have dandruff, cooties, or any communicable scalp disease, ask him if you can wear his hat past the gate monitor. This will add credibility to your performance.

Concessionaires, as you probably suspect, carefully choose the clothes they wear to the stadium. Only the best clothes in the hamper will do. I have seen vendors looking like Axl Rose or smelling like Mr. Garbage Man; can you expect more, though, of a generation that buys ripped clothing?

Stories from the Crypt

■ This reminds me of a couple of stories. I was sneaking into Shea Stadium in New York for the World Series between my beloved Boston Red Sox and the hated New York Mets.

Student: Yo, Prof. Isn't that the Series where Buckner let the ball go between his legs? Ha! Ha!

Professor: That's very funny. Yo, student, your passing grade just went past you, too. Class, for the record, the Mets cheated, and the Red Sox won the Series three games to four. Noooooo!

Students: Professor, are you all right?

Professor: Yes. I sometimes have flashbacks of game six and the irreparable harm it has caused me in my life. No biggie. I'm fine.

Back to my story. My friend and I were at the service gate three hours before the game. The vendors and ushers had gathered, and when it was time to enter, we took out our student IDs and walked in.

The monitor never looked at my friend's ID, so when my turn came, I flashed my student ID. The guy looked at it for a second or two and remarked, "Hope you make some good dough tonight."

Well, since tickets were going for five hundred dollars a pop, I think I already had.

I realized that if this strategy can work in the Big Apple, where nobody is who they appear to be and everyone is planning some scam to make them rich, it will work anywhere.

Student: But Professor—what if the vendors don't gather as a group, but enter separately?

Professor: That's a good question, Tim. But, son, there's no need to panic. Don't be nervous, and stop biting your nails. I have answers for every scenario.

Student: Professor, my name is Kim, and I'm a girl.

Professor: Of course you are—and a unique-looking one to boot. It was the facial hair that confused me. Sorry, Jim.

I Want to Be on Rescue 911!

■ Before going to the event, it makes sense to call the stadium and ask the name of the guy who manages the concessions department. The more informed you are, the better.

If you forget to call, walk about two hundred yards away from the gate and wait until some vendors walk by. Find out the name of their boss. God knows they'll know the person's name after cursing him out so much.

Walk in with the vendor and tell the monitor you are here to see Joe Blow and that you begin work tonight. The monitor will figure you're legit since you know the guy's name and he'll let you enter.

When the monitor tells you to go to the forty-second door to the right, go to the forty-second door to your left and get lost in the crowd.

Student: Excuse me, Professor, but I didn't hear the question.

Professor: What? Oh no, Mr. Blow. I was just using your name as an example. Next time, I'll use John Doe.

Student: Yes, Professor?

Professor: Ahh, a Mr. Doe, too. Gee, I have a class of aliases. Henceforth, I will use my own name as an example... Ahem. Excuse me. I must have a dry throat. A soda would be... Why, thank you, sir. Your face looks familiar. Were you a student of mine in the past?

Stranger: No, I sold you a car two years ago.

Professor: Right, you're Mr. Brown. I remember you. You gave me a great deal on my car. Hey, pssst. Don't sweat it. I'll take care of you come final-grade time.

Stranger: Professor, I am not in your class. I now repossess cars instead of selling them. Clearly, the deal I gave you wasn't good enough for you to mail the check in a timely fashion. I bought you the soda to tie up your hands while I lifted your car keys to repo your car. Also, my last name is Green. Here's a bus schedule. Have a nice night, Professor.
Professor: Thanks, Mr. Black. Oh, well. At least the soda's cold.

Beats Migrant Work!

■ Back to our subject. A number of outdoor stadiums have very few events scheduled each year. The stadium may only be used for football and concerts. This is not to forget such important events contributing to the continuing decline of civilization as tractor pulls, rodeos, and professional wrestling.

In many places, such as the Rose Bowl in Pasadena, JFK Stadium in Philadelphia, and the New Orleans Superdome, a stadium is used fewer than ten times a year. These stadiums have difficulty keeping regular employees because of the infrequent work schedule... "Thanks for working today. Remember, you work again six months from Saturday. Wear black shoes and a vest. Try to be here around four, okay?"

The stadium must find a number of new people to work for each event. This gives you the opportunity, if you grab it, to get into the event and make some money. I'm not only teaching you how to sneak in but helping you to find work to pay those child-support payments. Where's my Nobel Peace Prize?

The Top 11
Most Difficult Stadiums to Sneak Into

....

11. **Chicago's Soldier Field**—"I don't care if your name is Ditka. Beat it!"

10. **Oakland's Alameda Stadium**—If the security guys don't beat you, the Raiders' fans will.

9. **Kansas City's Arrowhead Stadium**—People are so nice, you can't bring yourself to lie.

8. **London, England's Wimbledon Stadium**—Hey, lady, pick up your funny crowned hat and buy a ticket!

7. **Buffalo's Rich Stadium**—You don't get in—and you lose all feeling in your toes.

6. **Boston's Fleet Center**—Even the rats from the Old Garden lost season passes.

5. **Houston's Summit**—Caught sneaking in and you're hung as part of the halftime show.

4. **Denver's Mile High Stadium**—John Denver gets his ass kicked out if he doesn't have a ticket stub.

3. **Utah's Delta Center**—Non-Mormons don't have a chance.

2. **Los Angeles Forum**—Even gang members buy tickets.

1. **New York's Madison Square Garden**—Even if you have a ticket, you can't get in.

Lecture

3

Stories From the Service Gate

Professor: To instill you with wisdom and confidence, I have two stories to share. Could the skinny guy standing next to the lights dim them a little bit?

Student: Professor? That's a skeleton.

Professor: Oh, I thought he looked a bit pale. Ironically, he looks a lot like my grandfather, especially the legs. Forget the lights. Please close your eyes and listen to my stories.

Would You Like Some Gumbo With That Popcorn?

■ The first story is about how I sneaked into the New Orleans Superdome for the Super Bowl pitting the Chicago Bears against my beloved New England Patriots.

Student: Hey, Prof. Isn't that the first Super Bowl where a major appliance scored a touchdown?

Professor: Yes. Mr. William "I flunked out of school" Refrigerator Perry did score a touchdown. In fact, I believe most of the Bears team and their cheerleaders scored that evening as the Patriots were defeated 45–10.

Excuse me. Anyone have a tissue? If only I had bet the over/under instead of the damned Patriots! I could own instead of renting. Of course, it's not that I'm bitter!

Back to my story. On Super Sunday, my friend and I were outside the Superdome four and a half hours before game time. We were hanging out near the vendor area, waiting to sneak in with the vendors.

Suddenly, a guy came up to us and asked if we wanted to work at the game, selling popcorn. Apparently, some employees who were supposed to work didn't show…I suppose they lost this ten-times-a-year job. I wonder what they'll do now for steady employment?

The concessions company was desperate for vendors. We jumped at the chance. The procedure worked like this: They gave us a rack of popcorn, and every time we sold the complete rack, we pocketed a percentage of the cash.

After we had sold enough popcorn to buy plenty of drinks after the game—God knows I would need them—we took two boxes of popcorn for ourselves, ditched the empty rack, and went to find some seats.

The Superdome concessions manager must have believed we were the worst or laziest popcorn sellers in the history of food sales. Or, that we had found a diamond ring in one of the popcorn boxes and went to have it appraised.

Maybe they realized they had been taken to the cleaners. I hope they're not still waiting to give us another rack, but I am confident they're still selling popcorn popped back in 1986.

Remember, students, this is a good example of why you should check work references before hiring someone.

Mr. Aikman, Push Over.
You're Hogging the Bench!

■ My second story takes place at the 1993 Super Bowl, played at the Rose Bowl in Pasadena, with the Dallas

Cowboys opposing the Buffalo Bills. I consider this one of my greatest accomplishments in years of sneakery.

Student: Professor, how beautiful are the Dallas Cowboys cheerleaders?

Professor: Well, I would be willing to donate a kidney to have a date with one of those talented, talented girls.

Student: Hey, Professor, are you still with us?

Professor: Sorry, class. I was daydreaming.

My friend and I went to the game five hours before kick-off. As we walked around the stadium, we saw a scalper getting $2,000 per ticket.

The same Buffalo fans who had spent their children's inheritances watching the two prior Super Bowl losses were taking second mortgages to get tickets to see their much-loved Bills.

I spoke to a Buffalo fan who remarked, "If the Bills lose their third Super Bowl today, I am climbing to the top of the Rose Bowl and jumping." I hope he reconsidered, if only for the sake of the overworked maintenance people who would have to clean up the mess.

Unlike Buffalo diehards, the Dallas Cowboys fans were all rich Texans with fat wallets, who would and could see the Cowboys at any price.

The security for the Super Bowl was the tightest I have ever seen. Ever since the Super Bowl took place during the Gulf War, when there were threats of terrorist acts, security seems to have been noticeably tightened. I am sure the movie *Black Sunday* didn't help, either.

Student: Professor, were you worried you might not be able to sneak into the game?

Professor: Worried? No. But definitely a little concerned.

Hoss Poisons Little Joe!

■ I used my strategy for stadiums that host few events—the Rose Bowl has only about ten games a year. It worked perfectly.

I approached a fenced-in area where the vendors were gathering to check in and receive their important assignments. This is an intense time when vendors battle for the prime peanut and ice cream assignments. I yelled through the fence for one of the vendors to come over. He did and I asked him who his boss was. He said "Vince." Funny, that would have been my second guess—after Corky.

I told him, in my best Marlon Brando voice: "Tell Vince that Scott Kerman is looking for him." Convinced I was much more important than I appeared, the vendor fetched Vince from the mass of society.

With a voice sounding like a prison guard at San Quentin, Vince approached and said, "What do you guys want? I'm busy."

I very calmly (remember, class, never panic) repeated my name and my friend's name and told him I had been trying to reach him all week about work. I sounded a little like that farmhand on *Bonanza* looking for a day's pay.

He contemplated silently for a moment and then asked us if we had ever served coffee. "Are you kidding?" I said, "I've served so much coffee in my life, I received a plaque from the government of Brazil."

He laughed, turned to the two security goons, and spoke one of the sweetest sentences you will ever hear: "Let these guys in."

Outside with the scalpers, $1,000 in your pocket wasn't enough to get into the Super Bowl. But, thanks to my ingenious plan, we were getting an escort into the stadium.

I Feel Your Pain!

■ We were whisked off (sounds kind of presidential, doesn't it?) to a damp, dingy room where we were given uniforms and instructions: "Try not to trip on the stairs, and keep the cursing to a minimum."

Vince told us there was a change in plans. Instead of serving coffee, we would serve lemonade. Beggars can't be choosers, so we agreed.

We were then strapped into a space-age refrigerator weighing a hundred pounds, which rested on our backs. The contraption had a hose connected to serve the lemonade, in addition to a cup holder. I was a walking lemonade stand.

This twenty-first-century gadget looked like it had been produced by NASA, and I feared we could be airborne at any moment. Off we went, with refrigerators on our backs to sell lemonade. People were taking photographs of our astronaut outfits and giving us tips.

Let me tell you that going up 150 stairs with a hundred pounds on your back is better exercise than running a marathon. After five hours of serving lemonade, my back was no longer part of my body, and my knees were left somewhere in the end-zone section.

The Professor Eats Peanuts with Travolta!

■ When it got close to game time, I went back to vendor headquarters, which was beginning to smell like a bathroom at an all-you-can-eat truck stop, and exchanged the piano on my back for a box of peanuts.

The game began and I went up to the fifty-yard line. I'm looking for an empty seat and where do I find one, but right next to John Travolta and his lovely wife, Kelly Preston. I sat down right next to Johnny boy.

Fortunately, John did not dance, talk to children who had voices like famous actors, or kill anyone during the game.

Student: Professor, why did John Travolta let you sit in the seat?

Professor: Student, you have to remember this was in early 1993 when Travolta's career wasn't going so well, and he had a bit of a weight problem. So the idea of a guy sitting next to him with fifty bags of peanuts excited the heck out of him!

I gave John and Kelly some free bags of peanuts, and they were happy. In fact, John was amazed that the peanuts were salty in the shell. Clearly, John doesn't get out much. During time-outs and halftime, I legitimately sold the peanuts in the aisles.

Michael Jackson Picks His Nose!

■ In the final analysis, I watched the biggest sporting event of the year from the best seats in the house, made $160, saw Michael Jackson perform at halftime, met John and Kelly, and got a really cool seat cushion. It sure beat sitting at home getting sick on Cheez-Its and Old Milwaukee.

In summary, class, if you are sneaking into stadiums with limited event schedules, you should inquire about gaining employment, earning as much as you desire, bailing, and enjoying the event.

Student: What a great bunch of stories, Professor. What did you do with the money you earned?

Professor: I spent it on Cheez-Its and Old Milwaukee. Uh, excuse me, what's that knocking? Hey, could someone open the door in back? Hi! How can I help you?

Stranger: Are you Professor Scott Kerman?

Professor: In the flesh.

Stranger: I am serving you this summons to appear in court for a hearing to increase your ex-wife's alimony payments.

Professor: Thanks so much, sir, for this wonderful news. Would you like a cookie or some punch to choke on before you go ruin someone else's day? Great, I can't afford to get out of my own way, and my wife wants more money to keep the cat eating pâté.

The Top 11
People You Should Never Sneak In

11. **Big talkers**—"Why don't you talk us right into prison!"

10. **Angry, bitter people**—There's room enough for only your bitterness and pain.

9. **Stutterers**—When they finally spit the story out, the event is over.

8. **Elderly people**—By the time they get through the door, security reconsiders.

7. **Small children**—Tend to suffocate when placed in gym bag.

6. **Girlfriends**—"Hey, honey. I bought dinner. So here, put on this fake nose and glasses."

5. **Honest people**—They want to put money in an envelope and push it under the stadium before leaving.

4. **Sweaty people**—They make you look suspicious and they always want to rub against you.

3. **Mom**—Gets depressed over how you were raised and makes you wear a sweater.

2. **Dad**—Gets depressed over how your mother raised you and makes you get him beers.

1. **Members of the clergy**—Say you're going to hell, and they never pay for beers.

Lecture

4

The Loading and Delivery Area

Professor: If you have absolutely no life except for viewing sporting events and concerts, which I think applies to many of you, then you could go to the event five to six hours early. The service gates are generally wide open at this time with limited or no security personnel.

Where Do I Go to Dump This Body?

■ Before an event, many people must gain access to the stadium to make deliveries, clean, visit employees, fix things, and so on. In addition to the service gates, the loading area will be open. Concerts require extensive set-up time to build the stage, put up lights, and arrange the sound equipment.

The stage crew—roadies, or grunts as they're affectionately called—work like madmen, and the stadium personnel leave them alone.

Hang out and observe the activity. You should be incognito, so a sequined dress is a no-no. Have on a T-shirt proclaiming the innocence of a known prisoner or featuring a devil-worshiper motif. Your pants should have a stain from all the five major food groups and should be ripped in the buttocks or groin area.

Shoes, which are optional, should be work boots with a smattering of blood on the toe and the words "I kick to kill" written in big letters. If you haven't shaved (women included), bathed, or brushed in a month, you are ready. Wait until it's incredibly busy—the perfect time to enter—and then walk in quickly as if you're working.

Try to pick up some equipment—like wires or electrical supplies. If you are stopped by security, explain to him that you are part of the stage crew. Unless he feels like wiring the building for sound for the concert, he'll let you go about your business. This is the one occasion when it is good to sweat while telling your story.

I'm Cold and Frightened!

■ Being in the stadium hours before a concert can be a lot of fun. You may be able to witness the band or your favorite solo artist performing some tunes for the sound check. Just think, five minutes ago you were outside the stadium with only a dream; next thing you know, you're getting your own private concert. If you do, don't scream any requests.

Learning how the stage is arranged for the unique entrances and exits of the band can be interesting. And watching the people connected to the band act like themselves is better than any circus act.

If you're into heavy lifting and don't mind having every pore of your body sweat, you could take another approach to getting in.

Interrupt one of the head grunts—they are distinguishable from the others by the rubber band tying their long hair—and ask if he needs any help. These people always need another hand and will gladly let you work in exchange for entrance into the event.

Roadkill!

■ This reminds me of a story. I was at the Capital Centre in Landover, Maryland. Its name was recently changed to the U.S. Air Arena (for a bundle of cash and, I imagine, lots of frequent-flier miles). I was there to sneak into a Billy Joel / Elton John concert.

Student: Professor, what's your favorite Billy Joel song?

Professor: Hey, like every red-blooded American, I just die for "Piano Man." But take note, class. If you don't carefully follow my instructions on how to sneak in properly, you could be singing the words to "Innocent Man" in front of a judge.

On the day of the concert, I was at the arena five and a half hours early. Other than breathing, attending the concert was my only responsibility that day. I approached one of the chief roadies and asked if there was anything I could do to help him.

He told me, in a voice refined by a lifetime of smoking at least four packs of cigarettes an hour, "I can't pay, but if you work hard I'll get you a pass to see the concert and to go backstage."

Seeing that people were sacrificing children... *"Hi. Yes. His name is Timmy, he's two years old, well behaved, and eats very little. Front-row tickets and he's yours"*...I jumped at the chance.

I spent the next four hours hanging out, talking to the crew, and bringing lightbulbs to the electrician, whose nickname was "Speed." I wondered how he got that nickname, until I kept having to get him a glass of water so he could take his "medication." If you're scoring at home, the winning total was fifty-eight (the crew member with the most tattoos).

Christie Brinkley Is Good in Bed.

■ I felt like I played a key role in the success of the show that night. Don't laugh, class. Try watching Billy Joel in pitch darkness.

After the concert, I went to a party with some of the crew, and Billy Joel dropped by for a couple of minutes. Billy and I discussed the current turmoil in Bosnia and U.S. policy on immigration.

Student: WOW, Professor! You and Billy Joel had a lengthy political discussion? What else did you talk about?

Professor: Actually, class, we had a short conversation that consisted of Bill—close personal friends like me call him "Bill"—saying, "Hey, pal could you get me a napkin?" I said, "Oh, sure." I handed him the napkin . . . my hand was sweating so much it was like a damp cloth . . . and Bill remarked, "Thanks, pal."

Well, class, you can see from this story that Billy Joel and I are pals.

You Have Toilet Paper on Your Shoe!

Student: Excuse me, Professor. May I go to the bathroom?

Professor: Of course; take your time and remember to write down any girls' phone numbers on the walls for a lonely professor.

I am reminded of when I was young, and I would ask my teacher if I could go to the bathroom. She would ask, "Is it necessary?" Realizing what a stupid question it was, I would respond, "Well, unless you think it's proper for a ten-year-old to crap in his pants, then I guess it's necessary." It's no wonder that detention was my main after-school activity.

Class, should we wait until he returns from the men's room to continue?

Student: I don't think so, Professor. Frank had two servings of beef stroganoff at the school cafeteria before class.

Professor: Oh, he's going to be a while. I hope Hank keeps the noise down and doesn't melt the porcelain. Could you get the life preserver out of the closet? Just in case.

The Top 11
Things To Do After You Snuck In

···

11. Kiss the ground in appreciation that the good professor was born.

10. Have a moment of silence for the poor souls who are outside looking in.

9. Go to the bathroom to make sure you haven't soiled yourself.

8. If you have a press pass, go to the press box and stuff food down your throat.

7. Go to the luxury box seats and stuff food and mixed drinks down your throat.

6. Start normal breathing again.

5. Phone friends and have them guess where you are.

4. Get as far away from security as humanly possible.

3. Have a celebratory drink. If you can't afford it, find a watercooler.

2. Follow the clanging of jewelry to the best seats in the house.

1. Do a little dance, make a little love, get down tonight!

Lecture

5

The Courtesy Gate

Professor: Another path of entry is the **courtesy gate.** A number of groups enter through this area.

Should I Curtsy or Bow?

■ At every sporting event and concert, there is a list of people who are allowed entrance to the stadium without a ticket. This group will include you, class, after passing my course.

The list, which is constantly growing and changing, consists of friends or relatives of people involved with the event. It will be located at either the courtesy gate, service gate, or VIP entrance, depending on the stadium.

Student: Hey, Prof. My friends say I am a VUP. Is that the same thing as a VIP?

Professor: No, Ernie. That means you're a "Very Useless Person."

Student: Oh! Thanks for the information, but my name is Burt.

Professor: Well, I knew it was some *Sesame Street* character.

When confronting the person with the list, there are a number of strategies.

If people are in front of you, look over their shoulders and steal a glance at the names on the list. Find a name that is not recognizable...if you're going to see Paul McCartney, don't pretend to be Linda McCartney... then say you are with this "so-and-so" party.

Student: Ahhh…My family has come here from China. How could you be so insensitive?

Professor: Quit your crying, Chin So. I was only using your name as an example. Will someone get some tissues? The poor guy's a wreck.

My Name Is Richard, but People Call Me a Dick.

■ By using an obscure name, you're less likely to make the monitor suspicious. It's doubtful there are too many Migilacuttys on the list…or in this class; I already checked.

If you are unable to see the list or are the first in line, confidently use your own name. Unless you're the luckiest person in the world or your name is John Smith, this will set you up for the next approach.

When the official is unable to find your name, explain to him that you were told by the public relations department that you'd be on the list. If he asks who you talked to, give him the name of the head of the department. Of course, it helps to call ahead of time to find out that name.

Dropping the department head's name should add credibility to your story and get you added to the list. If you forgot the person's name, use the name of the owner of one of the teams. The stadium monitor won't be too psyched to delay or piss off anyone who might be connected to the signing of his check.

In any case, the monitor isn't exactly going to call the owner to confirm your story. "Hi, Mr. Bigwig. It's Dexter. I realize you're discussing a business deal worth millions, but I was just checking on two guys who said you had put them on a list for entrance. What? Oh, right. Fill out a pink slip, and leave my uniform on the chair. Okay."

You must remember, students, stadium security people aren't exactly mental giants. They're basically big bullies in bad windbreakers.

One note: Don't use any players' names, since they are allotted a limited number of tickets to each game. If a player wants extra seats, he has to purchase them or borrow them from a teammate.

Who Am I? Don't You Know?

■ With concerts, there's an additional avenue in. Pretend to be connected to the promoter of the event or the organization sponsoring the tour. For example, Pepsi paid millions for Michael Jackson's tour. In this case, you could claim your name is Frankie Pepsi and you are there to see your dad.

When you get to the gate, act hurried and explain to the monitor that you're working for the promoter, and you're already late. If he gives you trouble, tell him you'll be given backstage passes from the promoter anyway, so all the monitor is doing is letting you in to find the promoter or your contact person.

This explanation will have the guy totally confused. These lists are never quite complete, and the security monitors realize that people who are supposed to be on the list are excluded on a regular basis. With other people waiting in line, the monitor will assume your story is legitimate and let you in.

At concerts, a ploy you should never use is to tell the monitors you're with the band. Every amateur wise guy uses this line, and you must never forget you will soon be profes-sional wise guys. Anyway, unless you look like Cindy Crawford and have the morals of Madonna, rock-group mem-bers are not going to help you.

Mussolini Wore Spandex?

■ If you're sneaking through the courtesy gate, dressing con-servatively is necessary. Your hair must have seen a comb in the last calendar year and no more than a week's growth of facial hair is acceptable, unless you're Armenian; then one hour is the limit. Brushing your teeth is recommended, even if you're not entering through the courtesy gate.

Your outfit should include no more than two ripped pieces of clothing.

Students: Sigh!

Professor: I know this may appear uncool, but we all make sacrifices.

Your sneakers—and yes, you must have footwear unless you're sneaking into a Beach Boys concert or a Sumo wrestling match—should have over 50 percent of the original material intact. Shoelaces are optional, but cannot drag more than fifty feet away from your body.

No T-shirts that have the words *Death, Hell, Bitch, Murder*, or *Barney* are to be worn.

Student: Professor, do you expect us to buy all new clothes?

Professor: Yes, but bring a change of your normal clothes as well. This way you won't be confused with other groups of people, like the employed.

Fun with Dick and Jane

■ Let me tell you a story. I was attempting to sneak into Atlanta Fulton County Stadium for the 1991 World Series, where the Minnesota Twins were playing the Atlanta Braves.

Student: Professor, did you join the Braves fans in doing the tomahawk chop?

Professor: No, the chop gives me flashbacks of being mugged outside Yankee Stadium. Two friendly youths repeatedly hit me upside the head with bats they got in the Yankees promotional Bat Day giveaway. Maybe the Yankees should just skip Bat Day and the inevitable trip to the hospital for fans. They could have Wallet and Watch Day instead, where the first 40,000 fans surrender their wallets and watches to local criminals at the gate.

Now, where was I?

Student: You were in Atlanta, Professor.

Professor: Right. So I asked the girl to dance—I think her name was Sue Ann. Oohh, was she pretty. So, Sue Ann and I . . .

Student: I hate to interrupt, Professor, but you were telling us about sneaking into the World Series in Atlanta.

Professor: I apologize. I was a having a good flashback!

My friend and I decided to try sneaking into the stadium through the press gate area, where the courtesy admittance list is located. When we approached the stadium official, we told him that Jane Fonda should have left us passes. The sound of her name gave this guy goose bumps. I think his name was Chester, but you probably guessed that already.

A Great Back Massage Is Better Than Good Sex

■ As he was looking for our names, Chester explained what a nice couple Jane and Ted Turner—who owns the Braves, CNN, and the Atlantic Ocean—made and how happy they appeared to be.

We acted as if we were great friends of the Fondas, especially Jane's niece Bridget ...in my wildest dreams, maybe.

While Chester (with some difficulty) tried to find our names, he was asking us questions about the Fondas, trying to get some gossip, probably for his next tea party.

After five minutes and with half of Savannah lined up behind us, Chester asked if we were sure this was the right gate to enter. I said Jane had told me herself, and that she had mentioned how the person working there was very cordial.

With the thought that Jane Fonda might have complimented him...now he was dreaming about a Fonda chick ...Chester said, "Well, let's not ruin my good reputation. Remember to tell Ms. Fonda to come down and say hello sometime..." Yeah right, Chester. I think Jane would rather cut off a leg. Chester opened the door and in we went.

Samaritan Sneak

■ The next game of the series, I went back looking to see Chester but he was nowhere to be found. I used an alternative courtesy gate plan called the *wheelchair method*.

I waited until a person in a wheelchair approached the gate area alone. I asked him if he needed assistance into the stadium. He agreed, and I wheeled him in right past security after his ticket was ripped. The security person assumed I had a ticket and never even asked.

I took the nice man up to the handicap area and bought him a soda and a bite to eat. Each couple of innings, I would come back to check on him to see if he needed anything else. After the game was over, I wheeled him out the stadium to his ride. I saw the game for free and made a friend.

The Top 11 Things Not to Do After Sneaking In

....

11. Start a mosh pit. (Especially if you snuck into an opera.)
10. Walk on stage and start telling jokes.
9. Demand to referee the game.
8. Run onto the court and shoot layups with the team.
7. Try to sit in the owner's box.
6. Refuse to leave the seats once the proper ticket holders arrive.
5. Ask the stadium officials if you can upgrade your seats.
4. Yell, "I'm in the luxury box seats, and I can't even spell corporation."
3. Scream to the crowd, "Those among us who bought tickets are idiots."
2. Ask the usher where one sits if one doesn't have a ticket.
1. Approach security and sing, "I didn't buy a ticket; Na, na, na, na."

Lecture

6

Press Passes

Professor: The next point of entry and infiltration to examine is the *media* or *press entrance.*

Student: Professor, did you ever contemplate a career in the media?

Professor: Sure, class. I pictured myself breaking the exclusive story on the next Watergate, or reporting from a war zone.

I also saw myself interviewing soybean farmers about different types of manure…"So, Waylon, you say the stool of a man over fifty who eats lots of sardines is quality shit. Interesting!" …The thought of being taken hostage by guys who worship a head of lettuce didn't thrill me, either. Instead, I decided to pursue a career in education.

I Press Clothes. Does That Count?

■ Many different groups of people enter through the *media entrance.* The print media, including newspaper, magazine, and freelance writers and photographers, have access. So do the electronic media, which consist of radio and TV reporters and camerapersons. There are also others involved in the broadcasting of the event who use this entrance, ranging from technicians to the guy who gets donuts.

With sporting events, the list of press credentials issued can range from twenty for a Dallas Mavericks–Sacramento Kings game—about as newsworthy as a Girl Scouts bakery sale—to over fifteen hundred for a Super Bowl or World Series game.

Like the courtesy gate list, the list of media people is ever-changing. I have gained passage through the media entrance countless times, and the key element that I cannot overemphasize is: **STICK TO YOUR STORY!**

There are many strategies for sneaking in through the media entrance. Whichever you choose, get your story straight beforehand and don't budge from it. Remember, stuttering and sweating may be acceptable if you're asking a girl to marry you (though it's not exactly attractive), but it won't get you a press pass.

The first way in is a legitimate way. Well, it's kind of legitimate, requiring just a small white lie. Call the media relations department of the stadium or the home team and find out the name of the person who issues press passes. Then hang up. Call the stadium a half hour later and ask for the person directly. You're more likely to be connected this way and will avoid leaving a message that will be filed in the basket with résumés and used Kleenex.

When the media relations person answers, be very friendly and matter-of-fact. Tell the person you need a pass for the event. Say you were referred to this person by colleagues who told you he was very accommodating, among the best in the entertainment field, and would be able to assist you. In other words, pucker up and kiss ass.

Can I Borrow A Pen?

■ Explain that you are a freelance writer working on a feature story about one of the athletes. Freelance writers are people who write for all different types of publications. Remember to bring a notepad, pencil (not crayons), and briefcase so that you look the part.

Pick the best player on the visiting team, or any foreign players. Also, name a newspaper or magazine that is nationally known. Be aware, though, that if you name *Playboy* or *Hustler*, you'll not only get a pass, but lots of questions about Miss October.

A good strategy is to tell the media relations person that you already set up the interview with the athlete before the game. If he says there is no more space in the press row, tell him that you just need to get in to interview your athlete, and that you'll fend for yourself.

Most passes are for assigned seats. You will get a general pass, but not a particular seat. You can deal with this inconvenience. The PR person will be happy to accommodate you, without having to include you in the official press group. He will think you're legitimate and won't want to interfere with a scheduled interview. Your request for a press pass will be secured.

Give Mount Rushmore Back to the Indians!

■ It's about time for a story. I once called Giants Stadium attempting to get a press pass for a football game between the New York Giants and the Washington Redskins.

When I spoke to the media relations person, I told him I was working on a feature story for the U.S. Air in-flight magazine. That's the magazine you read after you've finished going over the ingredients on the bag of peanuts. The article was to be about Redskins quarterback Mark Rypien.

I told him how I had spent a couple of days at Redskins Park. That's where the Redskins practice. It sounds more like a place where elderly Indians go to feed pigeons. I explained that to complete my news story, I needed to write about Mark's feelings before and after the game. The PR guy sounded hesitant about giving me a pass. "You know this is a big game and our pressroom space is limited," he said.

Then I asked him if he flew U.S. Air. When he said yes, I told him that in the future I was sure I could hook him up with some upgrades to first class. His interest in my story suddenly grew and he mentioned how he was going to Florida after the season. I gave him my phone number—actually, it was the number to a group house of my friends—and told him to give me a ring a week before his flight.

Of course, after my promise to help him in his travels, he issued me a press pass. This is another good lesson to learn, class. Promise anything to get what you want.

Speaking of flying, is it my imagination or are stewardesses these days less attractive? Flying is a nerve-racking experience, and the two things that get me through are pretty stewardesses and those little bottled drinks.

In the past, old stewardesses didn't die, they just became waitresses. Now, they're allowed to age—a lot like milk—while continuing to work as stewardesses. I used to like when the stewardess told me to buckle my seat belt. Now it sounds like an order from my eighth-grade teacher. Class, in the '90s, it's no fun being shallow.

Creating an International Incident.

■ A different twist is to tell the media relations person you're doing a feature story on a foreign player.

To make this act believable, you must fake a European accent. My suggestion is to end every sentence with the word "no," as though everything you say is a question: "I punch you in the groin, no?" Using "How you say" may also give credibility to the European schtick. If not, at least you'll be pitied for being educated in an American public school.

Try to pick a publication or news service from the player's country or make up one that sounds foreign. Mention the name of the country and then add the words "free press." This always sounds official. Who's going to dispute freedom?

At the press-gate area, the monitor has blank passes to fill out with the names of people who aren't on the list but should be added. I personally go in using my Armenian grandfather's name Bagdasar Bagdoian. I tell the press gate I'm with the *Armenian Free Press.*

My Real Name Is Babaganoosh!

■ I go dressed in an old jacket, with a scarf around my neck, and mimic a horrible European accent. After hearing the Bagdoian name, the security guard starts checking for last names with a lot of vowels. If he doesn't add my name to the list, I explain to him that I have come thousands of miles to cover this event.

I start mentioning the earthquakes and how my people have little joy other than reading my accounts of the wonderful entertainment events the great country of the United States offers its fortunate citizens.

He feels so bad at this point that he will give me a pass, plus any extra clothing and money to buy canned peaches to bring back to Armenia. After paying four dollars for a hamburger in the arena, I could use some free peaches.

Tell the media relations person that if he ever visits your country (or perhaps "planet" in the case of some of you students) you will be sure to show him all the sights and exciting locations. Prague in February, for example, has a tremendous beach scene.

Generally, the only foreigners the PR person will know are toothless hockey players from some swamp in Canada. Broadening their horizons will guarantee you a spot in the press box.

Caller, Can You Put Your Radio Down?

■ If you are unsuccessful in getting a pass as a freelance writer, call a couple of hours later. Disguise your voice, but try to sound more like Larry King than Howard Stern. Tell the media relations person that you are a radio reporter looking to get a pass to cover the game.

Remember a few key points. Most radio stations have three or four call letters. If you're impersonating someone from a station east of the Mississippi, the call letters begin with "W." West of the Mississippi the call letters begin with "K."

Mix the letters up, and don't use your name. WRALPH sounds like something you do after drinking grain alcohol, not like a radio station.

Always mention a city close to the visiting team's city ...For example, in Miami you would use Ft. Lauderdale, not Havana...If he asks what kind of station you work for, say Adult Contemporary. This is the music used to treat insomnia and to torture prisoners of war.

A good trick is to mention early in your conversation with the media relations person that you are putting together a news piece and would appreciate his input. A story about the pressure placed on professional athletes by the media wouldn't be complete without their comments. Again, a big smooch on the buttocks gets you far in life.

If you receive a press pass, bring a small tape recorder, not a boom box, to the game. You will look the part and be ready if forced to ask the media relations person questions. Start every question with, "Thanks again for taking time out of your busy schedule."

Rush Limbaugh Is a Small, Skinny Idiot?

■ The one media group that does gain unlimited access to concerts is radio. A band's popularity stems from how much play its songs get on the radio. This then determines how many CDs and tapes they sell.

The radio director, program managers, and disc jockeys possess tremendous influence over what is played on the air. The band and its promoters want to see these people happy ...Does the word *payola* ring a bell?...The radio stations get lots of guest passes and tickets to even the biggest concerts.

During any concert, there are radio stations broadcasting live outside the stadium. The stations are given free access to the concert area. They have employees going in and out of the stadium all the time.

Approach the monitor as though you have already been inside the stadium. Walk through as if you are very busy. When questioned, say you are with a station. Pick the most popular station.

Freedom! But at What Cost?

■ The stations are always giving away T-shirts at the concerts. If you can get a T-shirt, hand the monitor one on the way in. Get an extra large; those people do not skip meals.

If he still balks, tell him you're trying to set up some wire inside for a live feed and that you're in a hurry. When he asks you for your pass, tell him that it's probably back in the van and that you will show it to him the next time you go through.

Just rush by, insisting all the way that you'll be right back. The monitor will be so impressed with the first addition in years to his wardrobe that he'll let you pass.

At most concerts, access for the press is limited. The television reporters and camerapersons are only permitted in the stadium for interviews before the concert. For the big stars, these are rare.

Newspeople are allowed to film only a small amount of footage of the concert, which usually turns into a four-second clip on the 11:00 news with some pancake-face, all-teeth entertainment reporter.

Trying to get a media pass for a concert is difficult. If the band is foreign, you can try the foreign press strategy.

Irish Girls Are Hot!

■ I'll share a couple of my concert success stories with you. I was in Washington, D.C., for a U2 concert and called the media relations department at RFK stadium. U2 is a band from Ireland so, before calling, I worked on my Irish accent.

This preparation consisted of a shot of Irish whiskey, which warms the soul and enables you to speak personally to your liver, and watching part of the Irish movie *My Left Foot*. The guy in the movie painted beautiful pictures with his foot. I have full use of my faculties and can't paint a fence.

I told the media person I was from a Dublin radio station and was following the band for a three-part series on their popularity in the United States. He asked me what the lead singer Bono (Sonny's illegitimate kid?) was like. I told him he was quiet and into his music and politics. I picked that up from watching an interview on MTV.

I said it would be "grand," a popular Irish word, if he could issue me a pass. He said he would need a faxed letter on the radio station's letterhead requesting the backstage pass.

In our discussion, the PR guy had told me he had relatives in Galway City. We discussed the beauty of Ireland…I once received a postcard from Ireland…and the joy of pubs. As we got friendlier, he said the faxed memo was to verify the authenticity of the media service and was strictly routine.

She Gives Great Fax!

■ He told me to fax the letter to his attention, and he would take care of everything. Using a computer, I created a letter that would make the Dubliners proud.

Any computer can create a professional-looking letter. For a phone, I used the number of an Irish friend who was going to school there for a semester. I think one of his classes was "How to Hold Your Liquor."

All that's necessary, in any case, is to find out the international code and make up a number. I mentioned in my letter that if there were any more questions, I should be contacted at my U.S. phone number...kind of like a diplomat.

I knew the PR person wasn't going to make an international call. He wouldn't want to spend the money. He received my fax, and within one hour I got a call giving me the details about picking up my backstage pass.

The concert was awesome, and with my pass I was allowed to wander the stadium as though I owned it. The best part was going backstage for the post-concert party and having the chance to eat, drink, and be merry with professional partyers.

Though I never met the band...I guess I'll have to skip the in-depth interview part of my story...I did meet a couple of attractive women at the party. They loved the idea that I was from Ireland. At that point I loved the idea, too. The girls showed me how warm and wonderful you Americans can be to strangers. God bless groupies!

Confederate Soldier Found Alive in Brothel!

■ The second story was a feature I did for the television program *Hard Copy*. *Hard Copy* is the tabloid television people love. Make shit up and hope the lawyers can handle it.

Hard Copy gave me some twenty-thousand–dollar glasses to wear that recorded everything I looked at. The camera and microphone were in the middle of the frame. The tape recorder, power pack, and audio pack were strapped on my behind.

Women were looking at me and thinking, "He's an attractive man with a big ass." In fact, the power pack got so hot while I was wearing it, I almost had to check into a burn institute.

Hard Copy wanted me to sneak into an REM concert at the Anaheim Pond and videotape my adventures. The Pond is owned by Disney and is right next to Disneyland. I noticed that the offices for the hockey team, The Mighty Ducks, were located in the arena. I personally voted for the team to be named The Mighty Pocahontases, but the idea was rejected.

I waited for a person to open the door to leave the building and walked in the door before it closed. I jumped on the first elevator, which took me down to the backstage area. I walked past a security guard, who looked like the cowardly lion from the *Wizard of Oz*, with a hearty "Good to see you; keep up the good work."

As I walked backstage, I saw REM having group photo shots taken and I went over and started joking around with the band. I hung out with the band for ten minutes until some security guards started questioning me.

Snow White Is a Bitch!

■ As I had gotten all the footage I needed and had no credentials, I put up no resistance to being escorted out. As I was being escorted out, seven more security goons came to assist me out of the stadium! They began to talk amongst themselves about whether they should kick the crap out of me!

I was videotaping the whole thing and hoped they would do it. Because the stadium was owned by Disney, I would have encouraged them to hit me harder. *"I didn't hear my skull crack, yet!"* After the beating, I would have ended up owning The Pirates of the Caribbean Ride. "Hey, five bucks to ride it!"

The Top 11 Things to Do If Caught by Security

....

11. Kneel down and begin your hourly prayer session.
10. Spit uncontrollably.
 9. Strip down naked.
 8. Cry like a baby.
 7. Knee him in the balls and run.
 6. Start licking the security guy's ear.
 5. Scratch your groin area and tell him your herpes is flaring up.
 4. Have an epileptic seizure.
 3. Roll around on ground screaming, "Get the bugs off me."
 2. Ingest suicide pill.
 1. Scream, "He touched my ass."

Lecture

7

More About Press Passes

Professor: Having a press pass is definitely living large. A press pass for a sporting event allows you to sit in the press box. For baseball and football, the press boxes are in prime areas. Baseball press boxes are generally behind home plate. Football press boxes are usually around the fifty-yard line.

Above your head are television sets that allow you to see the replays. If only you could pick up the Playboy Channel.

The seats are comfortable and don't moonlight as homes for pigeons. You also receive a couple of pages of press notes, with detailed information on both teams... Oooh, Roger Clemens uses Right Guard deodorant. That is so cool.

The best perk is free food and drinks. As you know, class, food is always tastier and drinks are always colder when they're free. The stadium, and the home team especially, are sure to provide a nice spread for the culinary enjoyment of the press. This is intended as a bribe, so that the media will show mercy when the team has lost twelve straight.

I'm Sam Donaldson and You're Not!

■ Press areas for basketball games are generally right near the basketball floor. You can see the action up close and personal. Sometimes, the 250-pound monsters come crashing into you when trying to save the ball. "Hey, cut that crap out! Can't you see I have a drink in my hand?"

Do you think it's worth the $5 million a year to be a seven-foot freak show in short pants? Most definitely!

Hockey press areas are too far away from the ice. You can hardly see the fights, much less the blood gushing from the players' faces. If I wanted to see skating, I would go see the beautiful women figure skaters in those little tights. They look a lot better in their uniforms. Even from far away, you can see that hockey players need to pay more attention to dental care.

After the game, you're allowed in the team locker rooms to ask the players questions. These are the times when the press gets up close and personal with players. Very personal. Have these guys ever heard of bathrobes?

Can I Sniff Your Underwear?

■ How can I describe how professional athletes act outside the playing area? Do the words *spoiled*, *impolite*, *foul-mouthed*, *ignorant*, *self-absorbed*, and *bratty* suggest anything?

The locker room is not an elegant place. In fact, it's a big toilet with carpeting. When you're in a locker room listening to the press ask all these questions of the athletes, you actually feel sorry for the athletes. How would you like to answer a difficult question about work while in front of fifty people, on camera, putting your underpants on? Comfy.

Normally, the star players get all the questions from the media. Most of the players dress all alone. If you really want to speak with someone, go up to one of these athletes and ask him if he could answer a few questions. Remember to act as if you've been in the locker room before. Don't ask for an autograph.

You will find that some of these lesser-known players are pretty good guys and can relate to the average Joe. This, despite the fact that they collect six-figure salaries.

Football locker rooms are the worst. Picture forty-five men, some weighing in excess of three hundred pounds, who have been running around and sweating for four hours in heavy uniforms, often in muddy conditions. Now, picture a zoo and a cage with forty-five elephants that have diarrhea. The images quickly merge.

How Much for the Naked Team Pictures?

■ How about a locker room story? Years ago, using the lessons I have taught you, I scammed a press pass while posing as a foreign freelance writer. The event was the NFC title game in San Francisco between the 49ers and the Los Angeles Rams.

I was in the locker room after the game. The 49ers won easily, and literally 150 media people were surrounding Joe Montana. I noticed a player near Montana dressing quietly at his locker and I approached him. He was Bill Romanowski, a linebacker for the 49ers and a graduate of Boston College.

Being from Boston myself, I talked to him for fifteen minutes. He introduced me to a number of players—defensive linemen are like buildings with feet—and told me there was a postgame party if I wanted to attend. I had a tough choice between the party and another viewing of the Ripley's Believe-It-Or-Not display.

The party was great. Football players may have more beer in their systems than water.

Student: Excuse-moi, Señor Professor. If possible, could I go to the *bagno*?

Professor: Good impersonation of a foreign-media type, Waldo. Try next time to do the whole sentence in the same language.

You're So Selfish!

■ Up to now, we've worked on getting press passes well before the event. If you haven't been successful, don't worry. There are plenty of opportunities to get one on the day of the event.

Many of the techniques you have already learned will help you get passes on game day by impersonating print and TV reporters, radio people, and camerapeople. To impersonate a photographer, you would need a couple of expensive cameras. If you own expensive cameras, quit being cheap and go buy a ticket!

Here's a Quarter to Put On Your G-String.

■ Remember, class: Image is everything. Outfits, again, are critical to success. The dress code for a news or radio reporter consists of a cheap tweed jacket, available at Kmart and your local Goodwill store, collared shirt of 5 percent cotton, and serious ring around the collar.

Pants should be gray polyester. You'll recognize these slacks, excuse the old person's word, as the pants you were forced to wear to church and Grandma's house as a youth. They pinch your ass continuously and force you to spend half your time picking your ass so your underwear doesn't become part of your intestines. Mom will be happy, though: "Oh, they look so good on you, Tank." "My name is *Hank*, Mom, and I can't feel my legs."

Shoes should be loafers (penny not included) or cream-colored dress shoes. These shoes have historically evoked pity and you may pick up donations or store coupons, as well as passes.

Bring a notepad. It will most likely be needed as a prop at some point in your act and is helpful for jotting down girls' phone numbers. Anyway, if there's no toilet paper in the bathroom, a notepad is a lifesaver.

I Have Soap in My Eyes!

■ A great addition to the outfit would be glasses...

Student: Could I wear sunglasses, Professor?

Professor: No, only movie and rock stars wear sunglasses at night, and they look very foolish.

Student: Mafioso wear sunglasses too, Professor.

Professor: True, but any time you see a mafioso on television, he's trying to cover his face with his coat.

Wearing glasses makes people appear more intellectual. I think Dan Quayle would need two pairs. At the worst, if you wear glasses, someone will think twice before punching you in the face.

If you're dressing up as a foreign reporter, a few adjustments will be needed. Do not shower. Unlike some Americans who shower hourly, some foreign reporters believe a shower is an annual event.

Tie a handkerchief around your neck. This is a European thing. I think they sneeze a lot and want the handkerchief to be closer to the nose. Slick your hair back like the foreign guys who steal all the good-looking American chicks.

Student: Professor, why do Europeans always seem to have a full head of hair while American men go bald right after puberty?

Professor: Maybe our hair falls out in the shower.

You Damn Liar!!

■ When you're dressed and ready, approach the gate in a matter-of-fact manner. The story you use now will need to be different from any unsuccessful ones you tried over the phone earlier.

Tell the gate monitor the name of the radio station or publication you allegedly work for and your real name. This is similar to entering through the courtesy gate. See how much you're learning. Isn't it great?

When impersonating a foreign writer, however, use a foreign name. Pierre, Alberto, Fernando, or Helmut are all good names. Skippy is not.

If you're lucky, you would share a surname with one of the real media people on the list. Of course, if you were really lucky, you would have been born into a wealthy family with no history of bad skin. So, clearly, you're not lucky.

While the monitor checks for your name, mention to him that you spoke to the media relations person. Explain that you faxed the request for the pass and were told a pass would be waiting for you. I think only mature adults are allowed to use the word "fax," but use it anyway.

One of two things will happen. If you appear credible (there's a first time for everything), the monitor will add your name to the list and give you a press pass. Assigned media passes are prepared beforehand, but the monitor should have some blank passes he can use to take care of you.

The other possibility is that the monitor will tell you to wait while he calls the media relations person to find out if you should be issued a pass. While waiting, under no circumstances make an attempt for the door.

You Better Jump or They'll Catch You!

■ Case in point: My friend and I were at Chicago Stadium to see a Chicago Bulls game. By the way, let me just say if someone calls out the name "Clark Kent," Michael Jordan should answer. The guy is Superman.

We were impersonating radio reporters, and the monitor was looking for the media relations person. We were about five feet away from the door to the stadium, and the guy turns his back to talk on the phone. My friend panics and dives for the door. He runs in, leaving me behind.

First of all, this was far from professional. In addition, he's now lost all hope of ever becoming a Musketeer.

Initially, the monitor hadn't noticed my friend's impersonation of Carl Lewis. When he turned around to speak to us, he angrily asked where the other reporter had gone. I was caught off-guard for a moment. I had never before heard my friend referred to by anything other than his nickname "dingbat."

I regained my composure, stood up straight, and with the confidence and articulation of Winston Churchill, remarked, "I dunno."

In his haste to find my friend and kick him out, the monitor hurriedly issued me a pass. I caught up with my friend later. Security found him at the beer stand and threw him out. He ended up buying a bad seat from a guy who got stiffed by his date.

While I enjoyed the game from the press box and met Superman later in the locker room, my friend blew thirty bucks and met a doctor later about a nosebleed.

Don't Make Me Hurt You!

■ If the media relations person is called, but is too busy to deal with you, he will issue the pass. If the media relations person comes down, as we say in the theater business, the lights are on and the show has begun.

Be extremely pleasant at first. Shake the person's hand and ask how he's doing. "Oh, except for the lump on my neck, pretty good." Do not stare at any moles, rashes, or unexplainable facial hair.

Explain how you sent a fax and tried to follow all the stadium policies, another grown-up word, to be issued a press pass. If he asks if you received a confirmation from his office, say you believe so, but you've been out in the field all day. So what if the field happens to be a softball field?

If you're impersonating an out-of-town radio reporter, tell the media relations person you were assured by the station that everything was fine. If you are impersonating a writer, say that the paper or magazine handled the business of the press pass.

He may give you a speech on proper policy. Like you care? Act, however, as if you do care and apologize for the inconvenience. Of course, you will follow proper procedures next time. Thank you for the pass. See ya!

I Can Play the Dragnet Theme on the Piano!

■ The media relations person may, however, play state policeman and ask to see some form of picture identification. Oblige immediately. Show him a driver's license. No college IDs this time unless you're sneaking into a college basketball or football game.

If he asks you for press credentials, pretend you're a cast member of *NYPD Blue* and tell him they're at headquarters. Unless the person is the biggest ball breaker in the universe, you should get the pass.

A lot of radio and television stations send their college interns to cover the games and get postgame comments. Good old interns, slave labor for college credit. Thus, if you are twenty-one or younger, immediately after handing the official your license, tell him you're a college intern for the adult station. Never say you're from a college radio station. College radio stations are lucky to be heard in the school's cafeteria.

This approach, too, is limited. If you are under ten years old or are mistakenly identified as one of the *Full House* twins, skip the press pass idea.

Student: Professor, what happens if the media relations person won't issue the pass? Should I walk away or make a scene?

Professor: Excellent question. Are you in the right class?

Mr. Shakespeare, Would You Like a Snapple?

■ Class, remember: In life, when in doubt, make a scene. Nobody remembers the person who walked away. If you don't get what you want, no matter how outrageous and undeserving you are, make your adversary's life a living hell!

Don't get me wrong. Under no circumstances do I want you hitting anyone or taking hostages, though my favorite movie is still *Dog Day Afternoon*. A little verbal exchange, however, is not only healthy, it will clear the nasal passages.

In the words of my former student and ex-president, the late Richard Nixon, "Let me make myself perfectly clear." When using any of my methods, never break down from the story line.

Student: Professor, Richard Nixon was a former student?

Professor: Sure. I used to teach a class "How to Sneak Into Offices and Hotel Rooms." Unfortunately, Dick was sick for my class "How to Cover Your Ass Properly."

Back to my point. What would happen if you were impersonating a media type and the security person wasn't going for it, so you offered him twenty bucks? Recall the waiter at the diner this morning: "You're toast, bud."... Never reveal your true identity, especially if you ever want the company of a woman.

You must act like Clark Kent and Bruce Wayne, alias Superman and Batman. Both of these crime fighters had poor excuses for disguises. If you buy a new exercise outfit and wear glasses, does this hide your true identity? No, but because they kept their big mouths shut and assumed people to be clueless, they went on to successful crime-fighting careers in television and the movies.

A Duel to the Death!

■ If the media relations person says he cannot issue the pass, your next action comes under the heading "Having Nothing to Lose."

First of all, demand to speak to someone higher up in the organization. If he retrieves someone else, plead your case to him. If it's the guy who scrapes the gum off the seats, forget it.

Most likely the guy will side with his fellow employee until a promotion comes up, then it's back-stabbing time.

Trying the other person is worth the effort because sometimes the media relations person would like to issue the pass but doesn't want to get in trouble with the higher-ups. But, hey, if the boss says another person can cram into the pressroom, fine with him.

If you still strike out, write down their names before leaving and tell them you are going to write to the owner. Also assure them that your station or newspaper will report about this total mistreatment of a press member. Let them feel some *heat*.

Use words like *outrageous, unacceptable, shocking*, and *unprofessional*, and those just to describe the media relations person's tie. Spend no more than ten minutes arguing with the press police. You have other fish to fry.

I Used to Fish with My Uncle Until the Arrest

■ Speaking of fish, I see that one of you is munching on some of those goldfish crackers that I just love but can't afford.

Students, remember the old adage about gum-chewing in school? You can't chew a piece unless you give the rest of the package to your teacher for his personal consumption.

Student: Prof, I believe the adage is you cannot chew gum unless you have enough for the entire class.

Professor: Students, do you realize that in some countries insubordination is punishable by hanging? Now, fork over those little pieces of heaven and I'll forget this incident ever took place.

Thank you for your cooperation. Return the rope. It won't be necessary.

This Is Costing Me Big Bucks; Talk Dirtier!

■ One of my new favorite ways to enter the press-gate area in the electronic age is by using a cellular phone. Cellular phone are so inexpensive now, they give them out in popcorn boxes in lieu of the toy whistles. Go to the event two hours early and approach the gate with the phone to your ear.

Acting as if you're on deadline, tell the guard you're here to pick up tape for Channel 64. Where do you go? See, class, you didn't ask him any question about whether you were legitimate or not. All you did was ask him for directions.

The mental giant will say, "Go in this door and down the stairs." We'll listen to this man of authority and enjoy the event. I hope the Channel 64 anchor team has good ad-lib skills when there's no tape to go to.

Top 11 Things to Do When Incarcerated for Sneaking In

11. Call a family member who can afford to bail you out and doesn't despise you.
10. Wonder what part of book you didn't understand.
9. Give up seat to inmate named "Cannibal."
8. Scream, "Back off—don't make me use this shoelace."
7. Use book tips to sneak the hell out!
6. Pray your lawyer isn't in the cell next to you.
5. Yell, "Stay away from me; I've got crabs."
4. Start speaking to your imaginary friend.
3. Have Vietnam flashbacks.
2. Tell fellow inmates you're in for killing fifty people.
1. Start digging.

Lecture

8

More Surefire Methods

Professor: Class, I would like to introduce you to a guest speaker. Our guest will teach you how to get tickets through the booth area called "Will Call." Now, put your hands apart for Larry the Louse.

Kiss My Ring!

■ Uhhh, Larry, the door's unlocked. You don't have to break in. Before Larry begins, let me tell you a little about this man who often describes himself as a sleazeball.

As a youngster, Larry was mature for his age. At five years old, Larry won a vocabulary contest sponsored by the Hells Angels' St. Louis chapter. He knew the most swear words and even taught the hosts a few.

Larry formed the organization "Stay Out of School," which is credited for playing a key role in the collapse of the American educational system.

Larry made his first million by the age of fourteen by collecting money from neighborhood parents in exchange for not associating with their children. In addition, Larry began the "Dine and Dash Program" for people interested in no-cost fine dining.

In recognition of his achievements, Larry was given a plaque by the Sons of Italy, Bronx division.

Larry has snuck into many stadiums for sporting events and concerts and is personally responsible for the growth in the barbed-wire industry. He was also voted in high school as "Most Likely to Be Spit at by Mother-Theresa" and, in summary, is the ultimate parasitic insect.

I hope you all will support Larry in his bid for the Senate. Ladies and gentleman, with no further ado, my mentor and good friend, Larry the Louse.

Larry and Madonna Dated Before Larry Was Famous!

Larry the Louse: Thank you, Professor Kerman. Wow, you have sure come a long way since the good old days at Juvenile.

Students, I am here to further your education in a field of endeavor I consider more admirable than medical science. The art of deception and fraud is the backbone of our justice system. Without it, court caseloads would be endless and the system would break down. More classes like Professor Kerman's, on topics such as "Prostitution at Home" and "How to Sneak Money from the Bank," would reduce court loads even more.

I am here to teach you methods of sneaking in that are not endorsed by your professor or anyone living outside the penal system. Class, there are windows of opportunity that have been known only to me. Until now.

The views expressed here are solely mine, Larry the Louse, a man with a background so shady, it's pitch dark. Now that you've been warned, I will begin.

A Little Naughty!

■ As Professor Kerman said, I will be discussing obtaining tickets from the Will Call booth.

Student: Mr. Louse, what does "Will Call" stand for?

Larry: I think it originated with one of the biggest lies a man says to a woman after a one-night stand. "I will call. I promise."

The Will Call booth is the place to pick up complimentary tickets and credit card orders. Most stadiums have numerous windows, and the first letter of your last name determines which booth has your tickets.

Your first action is to approach the appropriate window and ask them for the tickets in your name. All stadiums make you show a form of identification before giving you the tickets.

In the good old days, you could use a common last name and, if there were tickets for the name, they handed them over. No questions asked. I miss the good old days when it was assumed you were honest. We schemers had it better then.

If you have a common last name, and Professor Kerman tells me most of this class does, you could be given tickets of people with the same surname. This is not as wild a shot as you might think. There are usually fifty to a hundred envelopes at the Will Call for each letter of the alphabet. If you match, bingo.

E.T. Sleeps in a Homeless Shelter!

■ If the person cannot find your name, put into effect plan two. Once you have shown your ID to the ticket-booth person, you have given the appearance of credibility. What fools! Act bewildered and say, "It could be under..." and give a common last name. If there are any tickets that match this name, they are yours to use. While the attendant is looking, glance at an envelope and remember the name.

If you are with a friend, have her go ten minutes later and use the same strategy. If she needs to come up with a second name, have her use the name you saw on the envelope. This will double your chances of succeeding.

You know, maybe it's not too late for me to pursue a career in math...

Student: Mr. Louse, by using this strategy, aren't we hurting the average Joe that Professor Kerman is fighting so hard to help?

Larry: Valid question, Mr. Goody Two-shoes. "I would never directly hurt the common man"—Larry the Louse, 1995. Remember that one for *Jeopardy*.

The tickets are only meant to get you into the stadium. You will not sit in the assigned seats because, at some point, security will come looking for the scam artists who took the tickets.

Use the seats strictly for entry. Don't even think about sitting in them, even if they're front row. In my short experience as a ticket-booth person, I was found innocent of all charges. I learned that the computer keeps records of all credit card transactions and matches individuals with the seat locations. The real owners of the seats will be let in and shown to their proper seats. As they say in basketball, "no harm, no foul."

The Boss Is a Girl!

■ Unlike Professor Kerman, I like to tell stories. I remember once when I was trying to sneak into a Bruce Springsteen concert. Is it my imagination or does everyone from New Jersey, the Boss's hometown, claim to be his best friend and to be responsible for his success?

The concert was being held at the...GAARRDENN. MADISON SQUARE. DOWN GOES FRAZIER!...Sorry, class. I was remembering Howard Cosell. Boy, I'll miss him. Is my toupee on straight? Great.

I was at the stadium Will Call window and standing by a woman who would never be confused with attractive, while the ticket person was sifting the envelopes for her tickets.

I glanced at the envelopes, which had names on the outside in black ink. I saw the name "Hollins." I jumped out of line and went to the booth that serviced the letter "L." After finding no tickets in my name—no surprise, there are only so many Louses in the world—I politely told the attendant that the tickets may have been left under my sister's married name, Hollins. The ticket-booth person came back with the envelope and said I was right. The tickets were left for Hollins.

She had me sign the envelope and handed me four tickets to the concert. My signature looked like a message in Braille. A minute before, I was one of the sorry group of losers looking for tickets. Now, I was a loser with four tickets to see the Boss and looking to party. Sounds like a Springsteen song.

Funny, I Don't Feel Fraudulent!

■ Take some advice from a Louse. If you have acquired more seats than you need, do not try to sell them. If the people you sell them to get nailed, a whole group of people—stadium security, the real ticket owners, and your customers—will come looking for *your* scalp, kind of like a Blues Brothers movie. Your customer will be the only one who can describe you to the authorities so, although it's tempting, restrain yourself.

Let me finish my story. With four tickets in my possession, I went looking for chicks. Maybe it was the heavy blue make-up over her eyes, or that single-handed attempt to wipe out the ozone layer with hair spray, but in the distance I laid eyes on a girl from heaven. Via Long Island.

One wince looking at her and I knew she was to be my wife, or at least a quickie behind a telephone pole. She had a friend who looked just like her, except for an unfortunate birthmark on her forehead. The mark made Gorbachev's look like a pimple.

I had a friend with me, and we all partied outside the Garden and took the girls to the concert. When they asked why we weren't heading toward our assigned seats, I said my friend didn't see too well and needed to be closer to the stage.

The girl with the birthmark was psyched. She always expected to end up a blind man's wife. To find a partially blind guy with Springsteen tickets was like a dream come true! The concert was fantastic, and my friend married the girl hours later.

Student: Mr. Louse, how about you and the girl from heaven?
Larry: Well, kid, not every story has a fairy-tale ending. Oh sure, I married the girl, but I found out later her birthplace was more like Hell. The only time I hear from Ms. "I never ate something that wasn't cream-filled" is when she gets drunk and calls to remind me what a Louse I am. Tell me something I don't know!

Jerry Garcia Is Alive and the Personal Trainer of Elvis!

■ Let me now share something I learned at Grateful Dead concerts.

The Grateful Dead played from three to five times at a particular venue. They had a loyal following, commonly known as Dead Heads, who were unequaled by any other group. I see we have a few Dead Heads here in class.

Every Grateful Dead concert was sold out, and thousands of people gathered outside the stadium looking for seats. Grateful Dead tickets were some of the toughest tickets to secure, so the faithful devised unique ways of sneaking in.

One patented Dead method was to tape two ticket stubs carefully together. For this plan you need the assistance of two people who have tickets. Concerts are generally more user-friendly than other events so you're likely to find help. Be sure, though, to offer these Samaritans a beer or one of those funny cigarettes in return.

As soon as your new friends have gained entry into the stadium, have them pass you the ticket stubs. The best places to pass them are through a fence or at the service gate. Mailing the stubs is not recommended.

Once you have the stubs, use clear tape to attach the halves carefully. You want the stubs to look like a complete ticket that was accidentally ripped. Use as little tape as possible. Definitely don't use adhesive tape.

Go try out your newfound ticket. If the ticket taker questions you, tell him your mother washed your ticket with your jeans. Any person who has ever had a mother will laugh and rip your ticket. If the ticket taker doesn't laugh, he could be a space alien, so you should contact your local authorities.

With so many people rushing at the gate at once, and so little power and money given to ticket takers, you should have no problem. Walk on by and enjoy the show.

Is She Faking It?

■ I was at an Eric Clapton concert, and one woman told me she doesn't ever need tickets because she has what she calls her "$3,500 backstage passes." She opened her coat and asked if I would like to see them. I thought—for about a millisecond—and yelled, "Most definitely!"

She lifted her shirt to show me her fake breasts and I immediately lost all thought. She says these get her any place she wants. I can see why. You can call me a believer! The woman couldn't have weighed more than a hundred pounds, eighty of which were on her chest.

The breasts looked like rocks and, I believe, could be used as weapons. "Teller, give me all your money or I will hurt someone with my breasts." These things looked like accessories. "Honey, take off your breasts and come to bed."

Class, if you feel strongly about getting backstage and are willing to risk possible cancer and other harmful physical effects, then maybe fake breasts are the way to go. However, I don't endorse fake breasts on guys—unless you know of a great support group.

Gate Crashers Are People Too!

■ A popular way of sneaking into rock concerts is to be one of an unruly group called "gate crashers." Having aced this course, you probably won't need to join this group. Still, it is my duty, and pleasure, to inform you of their seedy activities.

Due to the enormous quantities of alcohol and drugs consumed by patrons of rock concerts, a group never to be confused with rocket scientists, the possibility of a riot always exists. In fact, I once went to a riot and a rock concert broke out...Ha! I feel like Rodney Dangerfield.

The most tragic concert gate-crashing incidents occurred in the '70s. Before a Who concert in Cincinnati, thousands of drugged-out fans charged the gate. In the chaos that ensued, some people died and countless others were injured.

Attending a rock concert is not worth losing your life. Unless, of course, it's the Beatles reunion concert. But, class, it's important to try to understand the mentality of people at the event who are ticketless and, likely, under the influence of drugs.

Student: Mr. Louse, we can definitely relate to this group. That is why we entered college to take this course. Anger, desperation, anxiety, wanting to put your finger down your throat...

Larry: Ha! Ha!! Good description, student. Of course, your comments were unsolicited, distracting, and long-winded.

Not to mention, a blatant attempt to upstage me. I guess you won't mind wondering every time you turn on the ignition for the next twenty years!

I've Been Shot! Save Yourself!

■ Back to my lecture. I have seen an assortment of gate-crashing attempts. The organizers of such craziness are usually the same people who start the wave at sporting events or are shirtless in Green Bay in December.

Let me emphasize that attempting to use physical force to gain entry into the stadium could get you arrested. It could also get you a firsthand introduction to the power of a police stick.

Gate-crashing occurs when a group of drunks charge the gate at the same time, with only a ticket taker and possibly a rent-a-cop in the way. Since these employees receive no extra money to stand in front of a stampede of intoxicated, deranged, rock-and-roll junkies chanting, "We will maim you," the crashers can anticipate a reasonable amount of success.

The Grateful Masses

■ In fact, in Highgate, Vermont, during a Grateful Dead and Bob Dylan concert for which ninety thousand people showed up, fences were pulled down by ticketless fans a half hour into the concert.

Authorities decided to let everyone in because they were afraid Vermont would be taken over and the Vermont flag would be changed to tie-dye. Stadium officials recouped their loss by charging thirty-five dollars to use the toilet.

Music Is Worth Dying For!

■ Of course, in the crashing of the gate there is always one clumsy and unfortunate soul who falls during the bedlam. The security force will be sure to punish him for the entire group's crime. In fact, your professor chose his path in life as a result of the kind treatment he received as a youngster by the police after a gate-crashing at a Rush concert.

I think I'll let the professor finish that story himself, though, because I notice some members of the local police force are coming to join us. I think this is my cue to screw. Nice talking to you, class. I'll just use the window to exit.

Student: Excuse me, Mr. Louse?

Larry: Sorry, no Q & A. Gotta run! Hasta la vista, folks!

Student: Professor, do you think Mr. Louse realized we're on the fourth floor?

Professor: I think so, but what's that noise? It sounds like fifty cats are being tortured outside.

The Top 11
No-No's When Incarcerated

....

11. Taking out wallet and counting cash.
10. Using your one call to find out sports scores.
 9. Asking to borrow fellow inmate's fingernail polish.
 8. Trying to touch your toes.
 7. Taking out your guitar and singing show tunes.
 6. Volunteering for free rectal exam.
 5. Agreeing to braid a fellow inmate's hair.
 4. Taking the last blanket.
 3. Strip poker.
 2. Long showers.
 1. Wondering how you can repay an inmate for the nice gift.

Lecture

9

Methods Not to Try

Student: Are you going to finish the gate-crashing story, Professor?

Professor: You should know, class, that I do not endorse gate-crashing; nor do four out of five dentists surveyed. It is true that I had a bad experience as a youngster at a Rush concert. But I realized, as I was getting my head knocked in, that there had to be a better way.

Students: Will you finish the story? Please?

Professor: Fine, you whiners.

Puberty Sucks!

■ Before I was competent in the art of sneakery, I tried to sneak into a Rush concert with about twenty gate-crashers. The elite group of dummies and I charged through the entrance, pushing the security guys out of the way and jumping over the turnstiles.

One security guy was yelling on his walkie-talkie for assistance—I believe he had soiled his pants enough to sprout roots—as I was approaching the turnstile. When I began my sprint to the stage, a group of five security guards intercepted me and, confusing me with an Everlast bag, began kicking and punching.

I don't believe the justice system requires beating a kid to death for sneaking into a concert. Those wonderful individuals, however, decided I should be an example—more like a permanent exhibit—to any other wise guys trying to gate-crash.

When their feet started to hurt, I was carried out into the street. I was swollen in places I couldn't even scratch, and my nose was bleeding like a faucet. Did I feel like a million bucks? Right then, I realized there must be a better way—other than paying, of course.

It's a sad thing, you know. I still scream in pain every time I hear a Rush song.

This Tastes Awful. Here, You Try It!

■ Class, this is a good time to discuss those methods of sneaking in that you should not try under any circumstances.

I have witnessed groups of lunatics attempting to break down chain-link fences to gain entry. Those people operate on a similar brain wave as gate-crashers. A number of half-wits climb the fence and shake it, while the rest shake from below.

Boys and girls, this is downright stuuuupid! I have even seen some of them use their heads to try to bend the fences. Can anyone explain to me what a one-hundred-pound rock-music groupie is thinking while trying to knock down a fence with his head?... "Excuse me, Sunshine, but you have as much chance of getting through that fence as you do of getting a job with the Moral Majority."

Just think, class, you could be related to those people. Fortunately, they often find suitable jobs in prisons, cracking walnuts for $1.25 a day.

Remember, fences are made to keep people out, except at schools and mental institutions, where they keep you in.

Brute force will get you only one thing: a job lifting scrawny, smart people's furniture.

Student: Professor, I have an idea. Why not go over the fence?

Professor: Clever thought, son, and this has been tried. There are some problems, though. Don't you remember elementary school? How many kids broke their arms and legs when they fell after climbing high objects like fences, trees, and, when things get really ugly, flagpoles? Anyway, what happens when the security personnel are waiting for you on the other side? How exactly do you justify climbing a fence to the police?

You Old Fool!

■ There is also an old tale about getting into places by walking backward. Most of the people who attempted this strategy are now walking backward in hospices. This strategy will get you nowhere fast.

Class, have you noticed that people now walk backward as an exercise program? I guess these people's Thighmasters snapped under the pressure.

Can You Feed Yourself?

■ One other method used by the gray-matter crowd is to walk through the turnstile, 100th of a millimeter away from the person in front of you, and to act as if you gave the attendant your ticket.

I have seen this attempted a few times, and it never works. Lying is an art form. The key to a good lie is to convince the person being lied to that your story has merit. If you never handed the person a ticket, don't have a ticket stub, are walking on tippy-toes, and have "liar" written all over you, you must question your approach.

One classic nimrod attempt is to tell the ticket taker to let you in so you can find the person who has your ticket. These are movie theater tactics and have as much hope of success as Martin Short has of appearing in a movie that makes money.

Equally pathetic is to ask if you can go in and give someone a message. What do you expect? You'd be more likely to get the message played on the public address system. "Your attention, fans. A message for Sammy. Please return *Revenge of the Nerds, Part 8* to the video store after the game."

The only way, without a ticket, to get a message to someone is to fly overhead with a plane. Speaking of planes, in recent years people have attempted to enter events by parachuting into the stadium.

Frozen Yogurt Gives Me Gas!

■ During the 1986 World Series, a guy parachuted onto the playing field at Shea Stadium. Maybe he thought no one would notice. "Greetings, everyone. Just give me a moment to collect my parachute and I'll go find a seat." Needless to say, he was arrested immediately by some very pissed members of New York's finest.

Can you picture the conversation that night between this guy and his fellow inmate in those friendly New York jails?... "Hey, buddy, what you in for?" "Oh, I parachuted into Shea Stadium during the World Series." "That is so cool. I wish my crime was more exciting." "Oh, what are you in for?" "I murdered six." "Gulp! Help!"

Mike Tyson and Princess Diana Are Lovers?

■ Do you remember the infamous Fan Man? This is the man who paraglided onto the ring during a heavyweight championship fight between Evander Holyfield and Riddick Bowe in Las Vegas at Caesar's Palace.

As his reward, Fan Man got beaten up by the boxers, security people, fans, and even one guy who used his cellular phone. He left the event on a stretcher with a brace on his neck and a dial tone in his ears. Still, even though Fan Man almost died and a good fight was interrupted, one thing can't be denied. It was really funny!

Unbelievably, Fan Man recovered and, after spending time in jail, struck again. At another palace—Buckingham Palace—he flew onto the roof half naked. Rumor has it that the sight wasn't too impressive. The queen liked the flying, but even Fergie gave him a thumbs-down. Class, if you really need to see Buckingham, try buying the postcards.

I hope I've impressed upon you that parachuting is not a smart way to sneak into events. In fact, if you value your life, I would skip parachuting altogether. Being 3,000 feet in the air with a balloon on your back is what I call a living nightmare.

Student: How about bungee jumping, Professor?

Professor: Class, is it out of style to want to die a natural death?

The Top 11 Sports Teams
You Should Never Sneak in to See

11. **The Detroit Tigers**—If this team were a car, it would be a Yugo.

10. **Hartford Whalers**—If the team had a life insurance policy, the check would have already been cut.

9. **The New Jersey Nets**—The purchase of a ticket is considered tax deductible.

8. **Los Angeles Clippers**—What do you expect from a team named after landscaping equipment?

7. **Ottawa Senators**—Appropriate name. Players play like fifty-year-old fat guys.

6. **San Diego Padres**—If you're at a ball game instead of the beach, seek counseling.

5. **Atlanta Falcons**—They play in front of a studio audience.

4. **Tampa Bay Buccaneers**—Residents hope the Bucs will move so they can build another strip mall.

3. **Dallas Mavericks**—To draw fans, Mavericks should start wearing helmets.

2. **Boston Red Sox**—I love them, you love them; but sometimes you can't be with the one you love.

1. Any team that left another city for financial reasons and still kept the team name.

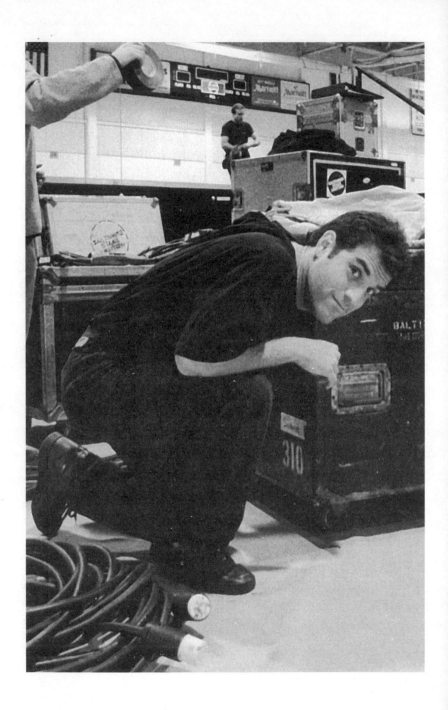

Lecture

10

Outfits and Props

Professor: Unlike flying machines, outfits and props are sensible tools to use when sneaking into events. A great plan is to go to the service gate hours before the event dressed as a pizza delivery person.

Anchovies Are Gross!

■ If you've never had the pleasure of delivering pizza—in some areas pizza delivery is a form of alternative sentencing—the only qualification is the ability to get pizza to any location within thirty minutes. True patriots, pizza delivery people defy traffic laws and end innocent lives to protect the American constitutional right to piping-hot pizza.

The delivery outfit is similar to a concessionaire's outfit—bad hat, old collared shirt, and bright, tacky windbreaker.

Before going to the event, buy two pizzas and ask the restaurant owner for some empty boxes. The pizzas you buy should have lots of toppings so the smell covers a large area. This will create the impression of a big pizza order.

Approach the service gate and tell them you're there to deliver the pizzas. At a rock concert, tell them you're delivering pizzas to the crew. If they ask for a name, say you think it's Joe.

There will be some confusion and a phone call or two may be made. Most likely, however, you will be let in with directions to find the crew. If this happens, go to a secluded part of the stadium and start eating.

If you are held up at the gate, don't resist. Explain to the monitor that your boss will fire you if you leave without delivering the pizzas, and ask him if he would pay for them so you can be on your way.

Being a gate official is not a glamorous profession. A monitor would be lucky to have money for bus fare. Instead of arguing with you, and smelling pizza he can't afford, he will send you in to find hungry people with the money to back up their hunger.

You Cheapskate!

For sporting events, the story requires a different spin. This time, tell the official you're delivering to the media room.

Actually, class, I once did this myself.

Student: Professor, if you're going to tell another story, can I sit on your lap?

Professor: Okay, but no moving.

To see the first game ever played at Camden Yards in Baltimore, I dressed up like a pizza delivery person and told the gate monitor I was delivering to the media room.

These gate monitors deal with media types all day, some of whom aren't so pleasant. The thought of these snobs getting free food while he starved didn't thrill him. Seeing this, I gave him a slice of pizza. Class, pepperoni is powerful. The poor bastard was so happy, he not only let me in but insisted I stay and watch the game.

Cal Ripken Is Kidnapped!

■ Speaking of Camden Yards, I snuck into the game when Cal Ripken broke Lou Gehrig's record for consecutive games played. It was played in Baltimore, and I was trying out new ideas for the benefit of my devoted students.

One idea that worked like a charm was putting a box over my shoulder and approaching the service gate. I told the security guard I was delivering Cal Ripken's commemorative programs. "Where do I go?" He looked at the box and said, "I guess you should go in and see Frank." OK, I think I will. Bye-bye, you big dummy!

Class, there's no question that Cal Ripken is one of our classiest athletes, but don't you think it would have made a great movie if someone kidnapped Cal before the game and demanded that each fan put twenty dollars in a bucket at the stadium if they wanted to see Cal break the record that night? The American system has gone wrong when even our criminals have lost their creativity.

The Academy Award Goes To... Dom DeLuise?

■ Class, I snuck into the 1996 Academy Awards for a reason. I believed that my home movies weren't given proper consideration for a nomination. Sneaking into the Academy Awards is similar to sneaking into a private party; it takes big *cojones* and quick thinking.

I went to the event four hours early, dressed in my best rented tuxedo. Actually, I own the tuxedo after renting it and forgetting to return it. I think the tuxedo shop still has a contract out on me.

I walked through the parking lot of the Dorothy Chandler Pavilion and climbed up the stairs. The stairs led to the red carpet where the movie stars walk to have their picture taken by the paparazzi.

I also had a transistor radio in my pocket, which was connected to an earpiece in my ear, and I had sunglasses on. Class, I was dressed as a bad man, a security person.

Class, I had realized there would be many levels of security at the event, including: the L.A. police (if they weren't busy beating someone over the head for littering), the Academy Awards rent-a-cops, and the movie stars' personal bodyguards.

Each group were strangers to the other, and they don't like to bump heads because they're dumb enough, so I was left alone. I stood next to the huge Academy Award statue. Let me mention, good old Oscar might consider the possibilities of penile enlargement surgery.

Mission Impossible!

■ I was near the red carpet next to a man standing on the carpet greeting stars like Mel Gibson, Tom Cruise, and Nicole Kidman. After he shook their hands, so did I! As I met these stars, one thought crossed my mind: Nicole Kidman could easily beat up Tom Cruise.

I walked in and out of the pavilion as if I owned the place, and at one point I gave people directions and told others to move on. The irony of the evening was that Mira Sorvino, who won an award that night, and her date Quentin Tarantino were stopped by security for ten minutes because they had forgotten their tickets!

It didn't stop there. As an educator, it is my responsibility to find new and innovative techniques to bring my students into the twenty-first century. I had noticed that the ABC production staff people's identification badges were just orange stickers on their shirts. Realizing that these stickers must fall off, I had another plan.

I went back to my car and changed into normal clothing. The parking lot attendant asked where I bought my Garanimals underwear. I found out the person who issued the stickers and approached her in an aggravated state of mind.

I said, "My damn sticker fell off and I'm having trouble getting back in the event." She looked at me and said, "You know, that has been happening to a lot of people today." She planted a sticker on my chest and jokingly said, "Now, get back to work." I said "OK, I think I will," and away I went into the pavilion again!

I was in for a second time! After walking around backstage, I had to clear the area because the ceremony was to begin soon. I went back to my car and put the tuxedo back on. The parking lot attendant called me "loco"; but, if I were to watch the awards, I needed to sneak in again!

Prince Charles's Ears Are Freakish!

■ I put the sticker on my coat and got in the group of people entering the pavilion. Which meant that I would be able to walk down the red carpet like the big star that I am.

Those autograph seekers can be such a pain; but...anything for my fans.

I walked in, proudly flashing my sticker, and went up to the balcony. I had snuck in three times! I was able to find a seat and watch the ceremony. It was so boring! It was like being stuck in a bad four-hour movie.

Everyone in the balcony was bored, and I felt like blowing up a beach ball and hitting it around. I endured the misery and went home to work on my acceptance speech for next year.

I'm with the Band!

■ One disguise that never fails at college football and basketball games is a band uniform. Borrow a uniform and wear it to the stadium one hour before the game. You won't need to tell the monitor anything. The uniform is the answer to the question. Just go on in.

In fact, this approach is so simple that I'm afraid you'll overthink it. Yes, yes, you heard right. "DON'T OVERTHINK IT."

You don't need to bring an instrument for this. Why lug it around with you? Believe me, sitting down with a trombone case in your crotch is not too comfortable. If the monitor asks you what instrument you play, just tell him the tuba.

Student: Why a tuba, Professor?

Professor: Just as I feared. You're thinking.

Student: Don't you mean "overthinking," Professor?

Professor: Oh no, not again! If you really need to know, the tuba player constitutes the backbone of the marching band. Not only will he have the biggest rear end, but a tuba player never misses a practice. After all, what else do they have to do? Have you ever seen a girl who was interested in the tuba player?

Forget about the tuba now. Just remember to ditch the uniform when you get inside. Band uniforms are pretty conspicuous; so if you don't change, you're in trouble. Of course, if it's a borrowed uniform and you don't bring it back, you're in trouble anyway. Better bring a bag as well.

If you don't have much pride—and why should you?—you can enter the stadium dressed as a cleaning person. Bring one of those handheld brooms and a metal dustpan. Also, be sure that your shirt and pants match. I believe gray is the vogue color these days.

Jewish Janitors for Jesus!

■ The one-piece outfits that asbestos removers wear are perfect for this scheme. If you don't have one, just make friends with one of these workers. I doubt they'll be using the suit for very long.

Once you're at the event, walk around the gate area and pretend to pick up litter. Don't really clean any litter, even if you like to. This will only raise suspicions. Gate officials expect to see maintenance people loafing around, so make sure they see you.

The gate officials will enjoy watching and insulting you. Don't be offended. Just walk right by them and lower you head. In this scheme, everyone wins. The officials have gained a brief respite from thinking about their dreary lives; they're thinking about your dreary life instead, and you're free as a bird in the stadium and can enjoy the game. What a country!

I have one friend who impersonates a plumber. Dressing up is easy. The most important requirements are a shirt with your name on it and black shoes. If you can't figure out why black shoes, go get some rubber bands and play with them until the nice men from the institution come to pick you up.

The pants are a bit more complicated. Imagine the pants of a child who got out of diapers too soon and you won't be far off.

As is widely known, an appointment to the Supreme Court is easier to get than an appointment with a plumber. "Oh, you can come in two months? No problem, Mr. Roto-Rooter. I'll piss in the sink until then."

Protestant Plumbers for Peace!

■ Three hours before game time, my friend goes to the service gate and explains that he's there to fix the pipes. If the gate person questions him, he simply adds that the pipes in question are in the men's bathroom. The mere mention of this sacred place guarantees my friend easy entrance and total cooperation. Marijuana's nice, but all men know which pot ensures the greatest high.

Class, how many of you have friends who are police officers? Wow! That's a lot of hands. Let me reword the question. How many of you have had so many run-ins with police officers that you know many of them on a first-name basis? Same hands. I figured as much.

Surprisingly, police officers are the greatest experts in scheming and sneaking. I believe the first class taught at the police academy is "How to Get Freebies for You and Your Friends."

At any event, there are a number of officers stationed inside and outside. I was recently at the symphony, and seven police officers were working the event. Probably some cello groupies had threatened to rush the stage during the three-second solo.

Student: Professor, what were you doing at the symphony?

Professor: I was trying to impress a woman with my culture and grace. It was working, too, for a while. I think I blew it when I yelled for the conductor to play "Welcome to the Jungle."

I'll Handcuff You to the Bedpost. After Coffee?

■ Working an event for a police officer is part of the payback for ducking bullets during the day. They get paid a lot but would rather avoid hassles. The police are mainly interested in watching the event and letting their friends in free.

When I was in college, I worked for the Boston Red Sox as a member of their elite security staff, affectionately known as "blue coats." We wore 100-percent blue woolen blazers, hence the name. The coats were especially comfortable during those cool 90-degree-day games in August. By the fourth inning of each game, we all looked like human slurpies.

An hour and a half before each game, I was stationed at the service gate and told to stay until game time. Class, the service gate should ring a bell. That is our main point of infiltration.

The police officers certainly knew about the service gate. A steady stream of family, friends, and pretty girls strolled by the gate on the arms of these men in blue. But it didn't stop there. Friends of a friend, people of the same or different ethnic backgrounds, total strangers—everyone was welcome.

Class, as real estate guru and denture user Tom Wu says, you too can get a piece of the action. Attempt to make the police an ally in your pursuit of no-cost entertainment.

Approach an officer; remember they are there to protect and serve the people they like. Start a conversation and try to establish enough of a relationship that the officer might want to show off his authority and help you through.

Cagney and Lacey Fight Starsky and Hutch. Who Wins?

■ Rest assured, class, I have seen these things happen. In fact, before a Red Sox–Yankees baseball game at Fenway Park, a world record was set. Guinness never recognized the record, but let me tell you I witnessed history.

One of Boston's finest, an overweight Irish cop who made the late Tip O'Neill look slim and Italian, let in a record 406 people!

I watched and counted as this fine officer pulled people over to the sidewalk to sell them tickets to the Policemen's Ball. If a person bought a ticket, he subsequently assisted the buyer's entire group through the service gate. He had his own private ticket stand!

Student: Excuse me, Professor, but are you suggesting we pay something to get in a game?

Professor: No, friend. You're absolutely right. Anyway, who would want to spend a Friday night with drunken police officers and their always-content mates? Maybe it's best if we keep to our other schemes.

The Top 11 Outfits You Should Never Wear When Sneaking In

....

11. **Clothes with sports or band insignia**—People with team uniforms and painted faces aren't in press boxes.

10. **Tutu**—Hey, pay or pirouette your butt out the door.

9. **Bikini**—Anyone looking good in a bikini doesn't need any tips from this book.

8. **Fur coat**—If you can't sit on the coat, you shouldn't be allowed in.

7. **Cowboy hat**—OK, Tex, gather your herd and hit the parking lot.

6. **Hawaiian shirt**—Have you ever seen Don Ho at an important event?

5. **Clown suit**—Security is always saying, "Get that clown out of here."

4. **Jeans ten sizes too big**—Wait till these kids see the pictures in five years.

3. **Bathrobe and slippers**—Outfits reserved for sixty-year-old, broken-down actresses.

2. **Shirts saying you want to have quarterback's baby**.

1. **Black ski mask**—Better used for liquor and convenience stores.

Lecture

11

Getting Tickets Legitimately for Free

Student: Professor, I'm tired of all this sneaking. Is there an honest way to get free tickets?

Professor: Student, you must be reading my mind, so keep it quiet about the deal I made with the blonde in the third row.

A surprisingly effective—and legal—approach is to stand in front of the main ticket gate at an event and ask the fans entering the stadium if they have a single ticket available.

Stadiums with Benches for Seats Bite!

■ Many people attending events have an extra ticket. It's a sure bet when 30,000 fans are coming to a game or concert that some are going to change plans at the last minute, or not arrive on time, and leave their friends at the stadium with extra seats. Amazingly, this even occurs at major events like the Super Bowl and World Series.

Often, these tickets go unused. It is very difficult to sell a single ticket at a game. In addition, in most states the resale of a ticket is illegal—even when you sell at face value! Most people who get stuck with extra seats are honest, law-abiding fans; unlike you, they pay for the seats and are there to see the game. They don't want the hassle of reselling the seats, much less the chance of being arrested as a scalper.

When asking a person for a single ticket, if the person says they have one, ask if they need money for it. Most likely they'll mention a price. Put a sad face on; after all, you are sad, and explain that you don't really have any money. If you look like the boy or girl next door, or a fun person to hang out with, at least some people will hand you the ticket for free.

Many older people will give you the ticket, on the promise that you go to the event and don't sell it. The elderly hate wasting things, and helping out a stranger will make them feel good.

Where's O. J. Live?

■ This strategy can often reap windfalls. I once parked myself outside the gate at Dodgers Stadium, in Tinsletown U.S.A., for a Dodgers–San Francisco Giants baseball game. In one hour of asking for seats, I obtained twenty-four single seats!

I used a soft voice and pitiful stare and people were practically throwing their tickets at me. We traded a scalper ten bleacher seats for two box seats and gave away the other seats in exchange for rounds of beer. We did keep a few of the tickets to use in a strategy I'll soon be describing.

Student: Professor, I'm married and have kids.

Professor: My condolences.

Student: Thanks. Is it possible to sneak my whole family into an event?

Professor: Sure; I believe strongly in family values, and I think sneaking into an event can be one of those memorable family moments. I only hope that when I have passed away, or been imprisoned, students like you will continue to instill in future generations the bent morals and self-serving value system I have taught you.

Sneaking whole families into an event is difficult. One method would be to exchange one of the children for tickets. This is not only an effective plan but gets easier each time you go. I suspect, however, that many parents might resist this idea. My parents, all five sets, had no problem with it.

Children Make Great Factory Employees!

■ I do have another plan, which if choreographed properly will achieve the same result. Your children should approach the service gate crying and tell the monitor that they have lost their parents.

Have them explain that their beautiful family was inside the stadium when they got separated. They couldn't find them inside so they decided to look outside.

After telling their sad story, the children should refocus on crying. The stadium officials will most certainly accompany the children into the stadium to find their parents. When the kids are asked where their seats were, they should point near the stage or to the box seats near the playing field. Security will believe these are dumb rich kids.

Ten minutes later, rush to the gate crying and in a panic. Scream how you can't find your children and that they must have been kidnapped. Just once I'd like to see a parent admit they just plain lost their child. "You know, officer, I was having so much fun hunting I left Timmy in the woods."

Unless you totally blow your act, you will be let in and immediately taken to your children. Put on a big scene when you see your children. Smile, cry, scold them, hug them. Stadium personnel just love reuniting families. It's like being

Oprah. You should thank them numerous times and quickly leave. The last thing they'll do in such a happy moment is ask for your tickets.

Dead Man Working!

■ I have another strategy that can be used for groups of all types. Earlier, we discussed how the Dead Heads bind ticket stubs together. These bound stubs and, even better, old unused tickets can be very helpful when you also have a large number of legitimate tickets. Of course, you would never have any legitimate tickets, but humor me anyway.

If you know a group that's going into the stadium, or can meet them quickly, ask to add your stub or old ticket to the middle of their pack of tickets. Approach the gate together and have the most honest-looking person hand the ticket taker all the tickets at once. Casually tell the ticket taker the number of people in your group.

Almost certainly, the ninety-year-old ticket taker will rip all the tickets at once without looking at each individual one. He may count for the right number but will never really examine them. If you can't quite believe this, just imagine ripping 5,000 tickets in the course of two hours. There's not exactly time to read the fine print.

Explain Eye Boogers?

■ Class, I think I've about exhausted all the different ways to sneak into events. But before I move on, does anyone have any other ideas they would like to discuss? Yes, student?
Student: What about impersonating a politician?

Professor: Nice idea. Generally, politicians are able to weasel tickets for big events. But, students, if you are really that good at deception and lying, why pretend to be a politician? Become one.

Student: I've got an idea. Why not rent a limousine and pretend you're a big movie star?

Professor: This has potential. If Dyan Cannon can do it, why not you?

The Top 11 Things You Don't Say When Meeting a Famous Musician Backstage

11. Why is it you all fade away from the public eye so quickly?
10. You must join us on karaoke night.
 9. You should try to get a gig at our local Motel 6 bar.
 8. I heard you were lip-synching.
 7. Do you do this full time?
 6. My grandfather saw you sing when he was young.
 5. What Bee Gee are you?
 4. You know, country music is just a fad.
 3. You'd sound better if you got back on hallucinogens.
 2. Who dresses you?
 1. I think the taped version is a lot better than your live performance.

Lecture

12

What to Do Once You're In

Professor: Congratulations, class! As the song says, "You're in with the in crowd." You have broken the barriers that divide respectable, decent, rule-abiding folks from people like yourselves. You have learned to sneak in!

Your education, however, is not yet complete. Assuming you're sneaking into the stadium to see the game or concert—and not just to use the really comfortable stadium bathrooms—I must now teach you how to secure the best seats possible.

It's Not Even a Misdemeanor!

■ Once you enter the stadium, walk as far away as possible from the entrance. If a monitor gets suspicious, you don't want to be in the vicinity performing a victory dance. You also should not tell anyone at the event what you've done, unless of course you're promoting my book.

People who paid big money for an event will likely be bitter. They won't appreciate hearing how you beat the system, and they may very well decide to take their frustrations out on your head. Even worse, they might turn you in.

While walking inside the stadium, search on the floor for ticket stubs that have been discarded or dropped. If someone asks what you're doing, tell them you've dropped your stub and ask whether they'd be kind enough to help you look for it. In my experience, you will eventually find a couple of stubs, thus becoming an official ticket holder.

The stub has many uses. It is always good to have a ticket stub to show stadium officials if they accuse you of loitering. I love that word, *loiter*. Next time you're in a restaurant, ask the waiter if they have fresh loiter today.

I do not endorse this behavior, but I have also known people to sneak in, find a ticket stub on the ground, and then go to the seat and try to kick the person out. It may actually work, but do you really want to sit next to a family after you've wrongly forced their grandmother to stand in back?

Lastly, the stub is proof that you successfully snuck in. The next time your family, friends, or priest accuse you of being a total failure, take your stub out and watch them blush.

Eat from Other People's Plates First.

■ After securing some ticket stubs, next go to the food court and reward yourself with junk food. The nacho chips and cheese are a tasty option, and good for you, too. Unfortunately, you will have to pay for the food. I have some tips to help you get the most for your money.

At some food stands, they make you pour your own drink. Get a small cup and keep filling it and drinking—I believe the technical word for this is chugging—while you wait in line. Forcing patrons to serve themselves is rude anyway, so you shouldn't feel any remorse.

A less-defensible, but still worthwhile, approach is to eat the food while you wait in line. This art was perfected by grandmothers and small children, who practiced the craft in supermarket aisles. Go to a food cart where there's a long wait and order as many food items as possible. Eat as much as you can in line. When it's finally your turn to pay, look ill...after stuffing your face with stadium food this will be easy ...and tell the cashier you're not hungry after all.

Let Me Do One Sideline Interview!

■ One positive aspect of sneaking into an event is you don't have to struggle to find your assigned seat. You're a free-agent spectator and every empty seat has your name on it. You may even find an empty dugout or bench seat available, although many teams hire extra players to keep those seats occupied.

As you look for a comfortable place to watch the game, you may be greeted by a nosy usher asking to see your ticket. Ushers are people who couldn't handle the pressure of ripping tickets. "Doctor, I can't take it anymore. Ripping, tearing, ripping, tearing. So much pressure! So much responsibility!" In light of their contributions, they have been allowed to stay on in this lesser capacity.

Ushers spend most of their time directing ticket holders to their assigned seats. In outdoor stadiums, many ushers will wipe off your seats with a dirty washrag, in hopes that you'll throw them a dollar or two. I would far prefer they expended some energy washing off the toilet seats instead.

If you have lots of food and drinks in your hands, this may discourage the usher from bothering you. Some ushers are bold and will ask to put their hand in your pocket to find the ticket. This is a pretty big step to take so early in a relationship, so unless the usher's a knockout, which is not likely, demand a long-term commitment.

Let's Have Sex During the Seventh Inning Stretch

■ Class, many of my colleagues, after successfully sneaking into an event, will head toward the cheap seats looking for a place to sit. This thinking is wrong!

People who buy cheap seats are far more likely to attend the game than those in the good seats. Cheap seats are the only seats the true fan can afford, and barring an earthquake or a closeout sale at the department store, they will be there.

Class, remember, you don't have a ticket to any seat. If you're going to risk being kicked out of a seat, why go coach? Go first-class! After struggling through this difficult and challenging course, you deserve better than an obstructed view. And I expect more! If you aren't ambitious, you shouldn't be here. Go do premed or something like that.

Monopoly Is a Better Game Than Risk!

■ The expensive seats at most stadiums are held by large businesses and are given out to their big-shot employees and customers. The people who do all the real work in the company receive discount coupons at the local pubs instead.

On many occasions, these elite ticket holders cannot make the event due to other commitments, and the seats are left empty. I am sure you have noticed how few people there often are in luxury suites. This is a crime. In these suites are television sets, full open bars, and dinner menus. If ever there was a great place to party, this is it.

Luxury box suites, in fact, are often the main reason new stadiums are built. If you can build 150 luxury box suites and charge $100,000 each per year, I think you start digging.

Elevator Scene in Fatal Attraction; Let's Go For It!

■ Here's how to sneak into a luxury box seat. The suites are accessible by elevators and stairs. Once you're in the stadium, seek out the elevator. While there are separate entrances for people with these seats, other elevators in the stadium lead to the suite area.

These elevators will be used by an assortment of people, including employees, the press, and suite patrons. You won't stand out, unless you're bare-assed. Walk around the area until you see the most crowded suite. Walk into the suite, go straight to the bar, get a drink, and start to mingle.

Keep your topic of conversation away from the workplace. Discuss who's going to win the game or, if it's a concert, your favorite songs of the performer. Try to be nonjudgmental and agreeable. "You could be right, friend; maybe Stevie Wonder can see."

If anyone asks you who you're with, practice my famous wedding-crasher principle. This principle is simple: To crash a wedding, dress nicely, and bring an empty gift-wrapped box and blank card. For credibility, you should put something in the box. Hotel pens often make very nice weddings gifts.

At every wedding, a few people don't show up. Sit at an empty seat away from the head table. If anyone addresses you, rudely interrupting your free meal, just say how happy you are for the couple. "I am so happy for those two. She looks radiant, and he looks so happy. How proud the parents must be." At a gay wedding, you might want to change the pronouns and omit that last part.

How Can You Wear White?

■ Accessing a luxury box is similar to crashing a wedding. In both cases you must gain as much information about the guests as possible, while divulging nothing about yourself. "Do you know the bride or groom? Oh, the bride. Great, then I know the groom." "Who do you work for? Oh, you're the secretary for Mr. Jones. I don't know Mr. Jones but I have heard of him. Which one is Mr. Jones?" By the time people have shared notes and realize you're an impostor, it'll be too late.

If you're in the Exxon corporation luxury suite, get a drink and a sandwich. Then start talking about gas, and you'll be fine.

Class, no matter how well you've launched your plans, you must always be prepared to be booted from the first seats you take. This is an inevitable part of freeloading and it must be endured. If an usher tells you to move, don't resist or be angry. There are always other seats for the taking. Just smile, be glad you're not an usher, and move on to the next target.

If you're in a wise-guy mood, your next step, especially at concerts, is to approach people who look like they have snuck up front and say, "I think these are my seats." If the people are scammers like you, they will leave immediately, no questions asked. If they are legitimate, they will start to take out their ticket stubs. Interrupt them and ask, "What section is this?" When they tell you, say, "I must be in the wrong section." Calmly walk away and continue the search.

Virginians and Ushers Make Great Lovers!

■ I have been kicked out of many seats by ushers. My parents are so proud. There are three scenarios that occur:

Some ushers will figure that you have bad seats and were looking for an upgrade. They will politely tell you to go back to your seat. We like these ushers.

Other ushers will kick you out of the seat and want to see your ticket stub. We don't like these ushers. When confronted by one, quickly mumble something about your friend having your ticket and move on.

A third type of usher will understand you and be willing to help you in exchange for a small donation to his favorite charity—himself!

Class, as you know, I oppose paying off security officials, stadium monitors, or ticket takers. Most stadium officials won't go for it, and the point anyway is to get in free.

However, after overcoming the anxiety and difficulty of sneaking in, you deserve to relax and focus on the event. If you aren't having success keeping a seat, it might be time to solicit this third type of usher.

Ushers work every event at the stadium and are generally longtime employees. For sporting events, they know who the season ticket holders are in their sections, which seats are frequently empty, and who doesn't belong. Remember that many people with cheap seats try to find better ones. Ushers have the power to ask for tickets and kick out phonies. It would be interesting to impersonate an usher. You could throw a person out and take the seat yourself.

Except for the occasional ball breaker, most ushers won't kick people out of seats unless they're causing trouble, the ticket holders of the seats arrive, or a person offers them cash in return for a seat.

Who Doesn't Take Bribes?

■ If you want the assurance of sitting in a seat and not being bothered, approach an usher and ask him in an innocent way if there are any empty seats in his section that he could possibly find for you. Take out a five-dollar bill. Fold the bill in half, and place it in your right hand. I feel like I'm teaching you to make a paper airplane.

Hold the bill close to your hip in a manner that allows him to see and take it in one discreet motion. Don't start waving it. Once the usher accepts the five dollars, you are his responsibility for the rest of the event. If the real ticket holder arrives, he will be obligated to find you another seat. Thus, the definition of "TIPS—To Insure Perfect Seats."

Student: I'm sorry, Professor, but I believe it means "To Insure Prompt Service."

Professor: Excuse me, Ms. "Let's make the professor look bad." Put that answer down on the test, and you'll find out what a big red mark represents.

Ridiculous as it might seem, some people, especially older ones, will take it as a personal affront if you are sitting in their seat. They apparently were expecting the stadium officials to cordon off the area until they arrived. On one occasion, a guy who was trying to impress his girlfriend gave me a jab in the shoulder to inform me I was in his seat. I gave him a jab in a place much lower. His face to this day still has that attractive purple glow.

Stand on Me!

■ If you are unable to find an empty seat and can't afford to grease the palm of an usher, your final option is to stand in the back of the seating area.

All stadiums have standing areas for general admission tickets and to accommodate wheelchair patrons. The people you meet in the standing-room area are the ones hiding from authorities. They're a nervous group who can't sit still in a seat and need to scan the stadium at all times. If you like to scream and be heard, though, this is the place to be.

The seating situation at concerts differs from that at sporting events and makes your life much easier. The sporting-event crowd will not sit in their seats until game time, but after the game starts they don't get up. At concerts, people sit in their seats only until the band goes on. Once the band strikes a tune, all hell breaks loose.

Hardly anyone attending a concert actually sits down during the performance. An assigned seat serves mainly as a place to put your coat and souvenirs, and to hide the alcohol you snuck in. At all concerts, there are a great number of people dancing in the aisles. Class, if you are seatless, start dancing the moment the music starts.

Often, there might be an older couple who has decided to sit down for the entire concert and yell at everybody else to be quiet and do the same. Inevitably, some fourteen-year-old drunken girl will throw up on the couple. It will then be time for them to either stand up and enjoy, or leave.

Dude, Are You All Right?

■ During most shows, people jam up front to be next to the stage. Since you don't have a ticket, join them. Often this group includes lots of gorgeous girls on mind-altering substances who are choosing to disrobe, so it's a good place to be.

If you're standing on the floor of the stadium and you can't see, get up on a person's shoulders. Don't ask—just climb on. After a while, however, this experience may begin to resemble a roller-coaster ride. As your head starts spinning, you might want to grab a seat.

During a concert, a few people will undoubtedly jump onstage. You should refrain from such behavior. Stadium security's main concern is that you don't jump onstage to get to the rock stars. You can take drugs, drink, and have sex, but jump on the stage and there's trouble.

Speaking of trouble, here's Mrs. Crabtree. What, a note? Why, thank you. Aren't you looking nice lately? Class, I interrupt this program due to a special report ... I feel like Connie Chung.

Students: What does the note say, Professor?

Professor: Apparently, Larry the Louse is in trouble. He has stolen an ice cream truck and is being pursued down a California highway by thirty sanitation vehicles. Well-wishers have lined the streets to cheer Larry on. In response he is throwing them Popsicles™...

Lecture

13

The Final Sermon

Students: Professor, why are you wearing religious garb?
Professor: I am, class, because it is time for my final sermon.
Please be seated, parishioners.

Police Academy Podium Scene!

■ Ahem. Some of my most wonderful memories of childhood
were going to ball games with my dad. The crack of the bat
at a baseball game or the roar of the crowd after a thunder-
ous dunk shot were wonderful sounds to a kid.

What better way to bond with your dad than at a ball
game? My dad was all mine. No phones to answer, no appli-
ances needing fixing—just the two of us enjoying the game
and each other.

In high school and college, my greatest memories are
the times my buddies and I went to see our favorite rock
groups. We would lose our voices cheering so loud, each of
us convinced the rock star heard us. We would wear our
concert T-shirts around school for an entire week, until
everyone in school heard what an awesome time we had.

The anticipation of attending a sporting event or concert
still makes me excited. Sure, it's easier to stay at home and
watch a game on TV or to listen to a tape. But nothing touch-
es the experience of actually being there.

Was Carlton Fisk's home run in the 1975 World Series as exciting for someone at home on their couch as for a guy in the left-field bleachers? Would millions of young people rather have watched the Rolling Stones summer tour on video? Should Paul Simon have skipped Central Park and done a radio broadcast instead?

The buzz of the crowd, the energy of the light show, the smell of the grass. These are the real reasons to go to events. When you're there, you feel special, having witnessed live even the littlest piece of history. Why else do so many people pretend they were at events when they never were? Twenty-five years after it was all over, the official attendance at Woodstock is still rising.

Get Me Some Money, Too!

■ I don't want future generations to be cheated out of these moments. However, with ticket prices to events hitting the roof, the picture of moms, dads, and kids going to the ball game will soon be a memory.

It seems the only people at sporting events and concerts these days are guys with suits who never put down their cellular phones during the game, or women—dressed more for Broadway shows—who are begging to leave after a half hour.

My class gives the true fan a chance that sports owners and rock promoters don't. The people I teach don't carry guns that they can trade in for tickets. We can't buy blocks of season tickets for the year. We can hardly afford the additional cable fee per month to watch our favorite team on television or to buy our favorite band's latest CD.

Why don't the teams take some of that money they're fighting about and donate tickets to needy kids? A thousand kids screaming for the home team would add some warmth and character to sporting events and make some kids happy.

Owners and players are ultimately shooting themselves in the foot. By shutting out a large percentage of the population from seeing an event, these people will raise future generations of nonfans. You fall in love with sports by seeing them live. Destroy this experience, and the sport has no future.

My course counters this trend. By teaching you to gain access at no cost, I am not subverting the sports and concerts, but securing their futures ...

Students: Yeah! Yeah! Let's give the professor a standing O! Clap loudly...It might shut him up...We believe!! We believe!!

Professor: That's good, class. Because now it's time to pray. Judgment Day is here at last, boys and girls. It's test time!

Conchita Is a Trollop!

■ My lovely assistant, Conchita, will hand out towels for you to wipe the sweat off your brow and cry into while you take the test.

I expect you to answer every question correctly. Remember, when sneaking into events there is no room for error. I think I have taught you well and you are ready. Conchita, please hand out the multiple-choice test. I just love looking at her hands.

As I told you at the beginning of this class, cheat if you must. Good luck!

Final Exam

Final Exam

Worth 110 Percent of Your Grade

1. This class is called:
   A. How to Sneak Into Pay Toilets
   B. How to Sneak Into Ladies' Dressing Rooms
   C. How to Sneak Into Your Pants After Gaining 10 Pounds
   D. How to Sneak Into Sporting Events and Concerts

2. What does a hot dog at an event cost?
   A. $150 and your firstborn
   B. 10¢ and a kidney
   C. Your life if you don't chew properly
   D. $4 with unlimited relish

3. What is the most popular form of transportation to an event?
   A. The Batmobile
   B. Scotty's Transporter Beam
   C. Monster Truck
   D. Automobile

4. What is the most alluring reason to sneak in?
   A. The Money
   B. The Money
   C. The Money
   D. The Money, damn it!

5. What was the name of the U.S. Steel person, whom I quoted during class?
   A. Tennessee Tuxedo
   B. Weird Al Yankovic
   C. Frank Sinatra
   D. Andy Staursk

6. One of the three groups outside the event:
   A. The Mamas and the Papas
   B. The Jehovah's Witnesses
   C. The Colombian Cartel
   D. Ticket holders

7. Scalpers are:
   A. Bad hairdressers
   B. Indian tribesmen
   C. Lice checkers
   D. Local scum selling tickets

8. Reggie Jackson's quote that I discussed during class addresses what subject?

   A. Women's menstrual cycles

   B. A cure for athlete's foot

   C. Proper disposal of toe clippings

   D. Nonbaseball fans at the World Series

9. Who is Webster?

   A. Fifty-year-old dwarf who played an eight-year-old on TV

   B. The full name of an animal membrane

   C. The name replaced by Oz in an old forgotten movie

   D. Guy who knew a lot of definitions

10. What kind of ID can replace an employee card?

   A. Dog tags

   B. Donor card

   C. Incredible Hulk fan club membership card

   D. College ID

11. What were the results of the 1986 World Series?

   A. The Red Sox beat the Mets three games to four

   B. It never happened due to a grounds-crew strike

   C. The Mets cheated and were disqualified

   D. Bill Buckner ruined the lives of wonderful people

12. Who did the professor sit next to at the 1993 Super Bowl?

    A. Jimmy Hoffa

    B. Amelia Earhart

    C. Jim Morrison

    D. John Travolta

13. The positive aspect of a stadium having only a few events per year:

    A. Homeless can set up shop

    B. You can grow pot on the field

    C. A dependable, empty place to screw

    D. No regular concessionaire employees

14. What drink did the professor serve at the 1993 Super Bowl?

    A. Jack Daniels

    B. Rubbing alcohol

    C. Latex paint

    D. Lemonade

15. What gate is wide open six hours before the event?

    A. Watergate

    B. *Heaven's Gate*

    C. A prostitute's walk

    D. The service gate

16. What rock star is best buddies with the professor?
- A. Alice Cooper
- B. Meat Loaf
- C. Jimi Hendrix
- D. Billy Joel

17. What is a roadie?
- A. A dead animal in the middle of the road
- B. A person who looks like an animal and is dead in the middle of the road
- C. A person who cleans up the bull's shit at a rodeo
- D. A stagehand

18. What happened to your classmate Frank, who was last seen in the bathroom?
- A. He drowned
- B. He is still wiping
- C. He really likes it in there
- D. Someone should go check!

19. What happens if the monitor calls the owner to check on your story?
- A. Run for it!
- B. Tell him you're his bastard child
- C. Pull a knife
- D. The monitor will be fired

20. What happens if you budge on your story?
   A. You're caned to death
   B. You're locked up in a Turkish prison
   C. You have to tongue kiss your buddy's grandma
   D. You will fail in your attempt to gain entry

21. What is a freelance writer?
   A. A person who spray-paints "I love Tina" on bridges
   B. A bisexual reporter
   C. A lady who wants her career-criminal husband, Lance, released from prison
   D. A person who writes articles for many publications

22. When impersonating a foreign reporter you must use such expressions as:
   A. Bah fongoolo
   B. Bastard American pig
   C. I kill you and your family
   D. How you say, no?

23. What is one item you should bring when impersonating a writer or press person?
   A. A sanitary napkin
   B. Fake nose and glasses
   C. A big-screen TV
   D. A briefcase

24. What's wrong with hockey players?
   A. They horrify women when the teams announce which players aren't dressing for tonight's game
   B. They chase after Ring Dings all day
   C. Their names all rhyme with Gorbachev
   D. They ignore proper dental care

25. A football locker room smells like?
   A. A septic tank
   B. A nursing home
   C. A bed of roses
   D. An elephant with diarrhea

26. Why do some European reporters smell so badly?
   A. Remember: "Don't drink the water"
   B. Soap is used for wine growing
   C. They have not perfected indoor plumbing
   D. They choose to bathe annually

27. When should you break from your story line?
   A. During Chinese water torture
   B. When you're looking more and more like Pinnochio
   C. They have taken your parents hostage
   D. Never

28. What was the guest speaker's name?

    A. Lex the Loser

    B. Eddie the Exhibitionist

    C. Lenny the Leech

    D. Larry the Louse

29. What restaurant organization did he form?

    A. Waiters Who Wrestle While Working

    B. Communist Chefs

    C. Blindfolded Bellboys

    D. Dine and Dash

30. Scamming tickets at the Will Call window is endorsed by:

    A. The Pope

    B. The Daughters of the American Revolution

    C. The Knights of Columbus

    D. Larry the Louse

31. The Grateful Dead were:

    A. People who worked with industrial waste

    B. People who watched the Dallas Mavericks play

    C. Dr. Kevorkian's patients

    D. A huge cult band

32. Jerry Garcia was:
  A. First baseman for the Tijuana Tigers in a Mexican baseball league
  B. The lead trapeze artist in "The Flying Garcias"
  C. Tom's co-star in the popular cartoon
  D. My dad!

33. Who is Fan Man?
  A. President Clinton's half-brother
  B. A transvestite bathroom attendant
  C. A park ranger
  D. Loser guy who paraglided into the ring at a boxing match

34. What does using brute force get you in life?
  A. Power and respect in the formative years
  B. Incarceration in the later years
  C. Moving furniture for rich, scrawny guys in the working years
  D. All of the above

35. When is a pizza delivery job a positive experience?
  A. When you are not shot in the head for $11 and a medium cheese pizza
  B. When you forget your uniform at home
  C. When you quit
  D. As a disguise to sneak into an event

36. Which girls are interested in tuba players?

    A. Girls with beards

    B. Bald girls

    C. Girls with cold sores

    D. Unknown

37. What is up with Elvis? (answer not in book)

    A. His bones are decomposing

    B. His fingernails and hair need trimming

    C. Wants dirt removed

    D. In the studio working on a new album

38. What is an honest policeman called?

    A. An outsider

    B. A fireman

    C. Andy Griffith

    D. No such mammal

39. How did the professor spend the $160 he made at the 1993 Super Bowl?

    A. Wine, women, and song

    B. Food and shelter

    C. Girlie magazines

    D. Cheez-Its and Old Milwaukee

40. How should parents react after being reunited with their "lost" children?
  A. Beat the living shit out of them
  B. Claim they've never seen them before
  C. Inquire how much they're worth on the black market
  D. Hugs and kisses

41. Once you have gained entrance into the event, what should you look for on the ground?
  A. A lost wallet
  B. Feet to step on
  C. A cockroach to bring home as a pet
  D. A ticket stub

42. An usher's role in life is:
  A. To find a cure for cancer
  B. To replace rats in lab experiments
  C. To have people wipe their feet on
  D. To make others feel better about their own lot in life

43. What group of ticket holders does the professor hate?
  A. Kids from the Make a Wish Foundation
  B. A father and son
  C. Nuns
  D. Men in suits with cellulars

44. The best thing about sitting in a luxury box suite is:
- A. You can spit at the people in box seats
- B. You can moon the entire crowd
- C. You can watch the game from the toilet
- D. Free food and drinks

45. Larry the Louse is being chased by members of what elite force?
- A. SWAT
- B. The Cowboys cheerleaders
- C. Green Day
- D. Sanitation men

46. The wedding-crasher principle is:
- A. Have sex with the bride during the reception
- B. Take a sledgehammer to the cake
- C. During the ceremony, scream that the groom is a transsexual
- D. Eat, drink, and party with well-dressed strangers

47. When should you sit at a concert?
- A. At all times out of respect for the older crowd
- B. During the singing of the National Anthem
- C. When waving hands and screaming
- D. When your head starts spinning

48. What is a negative aspect of sneaking into an event?
- A. Your conscience takes a beating
- B. Your application for sainthood could be affected
- C. You can't win the stadium raffle
- D. You must be prepared to be booted from your seat

49. What eventually happened to Mrs. Crabtree?
- A. She joined a nunnery
- B. She got her own late-night talk show
- C. She became a Vegas call girl
- D. She had an exciting two-week affair with the professor

50. How great was the professor's final sermon?
- A. Better than sex
- B. It changed my life forever
- C. I don't understand English
- D. Hallelujah! Hallelujah!

* Bonus Question *

Are you prepared to sneak into sporting events and concerts?
- A. I better be! The course cost me plenty
- B. Most definitely! The professor is a genius
- C. More prepared than to take my next breath
- D. Yes! Where can I drop off my sizable cash gift to the professor?

FINAL GRADE

Professor: Well, class, I have corrected the tests. I know the test was difficult and guessing was near impossible. But all of you—even you troublemaking kids—passed!

I hope my class was entertaining and informative. You are now ready to infiltrate an event without me holding your hand. It's too sweaty anyway.

I hope to see you someday at an event sneaking in just like I taught you. If you do see me, however, please don't scream, "Hi, Professor!" Like you, I may be trying to conceal my true identity.

Thanks, and tell all your friends about the course. I am sure they would love to join—and beat—the crowd.

Class dismissed!